RANGERS IN THE GAP
ACT WITH COURAGE. NEVER SURRENDER.

RICHARD DREBERT

TABLE OF CONTENTS

DEDICATION

Before you read this book, I'd like to tell you why I invested in producing it and giving it to you.

The children of Burma have always been the most helpless with the most to lose in this struggle. The longest-standing civil war in recorded history continues to ravage the present generations and permanently mar the hearts and minds of Burma's children.

This legacy of decades of military rule has made Burma a nation where few children experience anything remotely close to what you and I want for our own children. Imagine your family growing up:

- as one of 5,000 child soldiers in the Burma Army
- facing a high — but preventable — mortality rate for lack of the most basic healthcare (Burma is ranked 189/194 in healthcare worldwide, spending just 4 percent of GDP on healthcare)
- where only 4 percent of children attend school (Burma spent just 1 percent of its GDP on education in 2011)
- as one of half a million people displaced by conflict

Despite signing cease-fires with most ethnic groups, more than half a million people remain internally displaced. Ongoing conflict in Kachin State alone saw

30,000 newly displaced people in 2012, and the destruction of villages continues to this day.

The tradition of human rights abuses by the Burma Army — including rape, torture, forced labor, landmines, confiscation of land and pillaging of natural resources — continues today.

With this in mind, I challenge you to consider the stories of these modern heroes — people not so different from you and me, people who want to create a legacy of love in a fallen world.

They embody what Jesus said in John 15:13, "Greater love has no one than this: to lay down one's life for one's friends."

You can learn more about Burma's children, and what my friends are doing to help them, by visiting: www.freeburmarangers.org and www.partnersworld.org.

This book is dedicated to these friends, my heroes.

Jeff Wall
CEO WISPERTEK

The book you are about to read is a compilation of authentic life stories. The facts are true, and the events are real. These storytellers have dealt with crisis, tragedy, abuse and neglect and have shared their most private moments, mess-ups and hang-ups in order for others to learn and grow from them. In order to protect the identities of those involved in their pasts, the names and details of some of the people mentioned in this book have been withheld or changed.

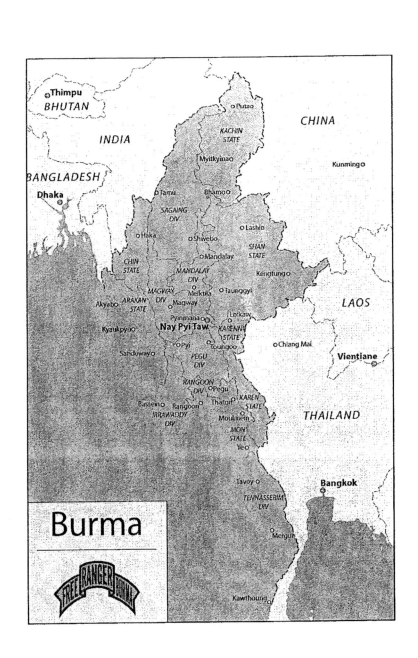

Burma

FROM THE WRITER

Free Burma Rangers travel in treacherous political territories. I have changed some names or nuanced scenes to keep from endangering individuals or families. Memories of exact conversations and events have receded over time, but we have endeavored to preserve the accuracy of each story and to bridge any language or memory gaps with culturally typical material.

To interview U.S. Army Major David Eubank (Special Forces Detachment Commander), Ret., I scaled his missionary odyssey in stages, like an ascent of Mount McKinley. Dave set his signature pace, and I didn't dare let him out of my sight, or I would have been *lost.*

At first, he contacted me by satellite transceiver while trekking in Burma with a Free Burma Rangers team. Weeks later we spoke by mobile phone as he jolted along the Burma border in his pickup. Finally, we interviewed for several hours between his meetings with ethnic Rangers — some who hiked weeks through Burma jungles to attend strategy sessions.

Karen Eubank — mother, teacher, writer, child evangelist and friend to thousands of supporters — spoke to me from the Free Burma Rangers headquarters. Karen's description of emotional currents that she and Dave forded together baptized each chapter of the book with gentle authenticity.

Months later, while the Eubank family itinerated in Alaska, we all met face to face. The children and I chatted about rodeos and pets: horses, pangolins and Burma monkeys. Sahale, Suuzanne and Peter are forces of nature, like Dave and Karen, and essential to an unfolding Eubank legacy that transcends words in any book.

As for Eliya, Sai Nawng, Doh Say, Ka Paw Say and Saw Sun, these men will live in my heart and prayers from now on. As I helped tell their stories, I marveled at God's mercy in each of their lives and in my own: Despite language obstacles, I needed an interpreter to translate during only *one* of the interviews.

After our conversations were finished, each Ranger vanished into the backcountry again, to train and lead their Free Burma Rangers teams.

These seven storytellers are trailblazers who brave landmines and bullets to bring help, hope and love to the people of Burma. Their book challenges readers to join in the battle to deliver relief to the one million internally displaced people (IDPs) living under an oppressive military dictatorship.

Two big thanks! First, to Free Burma Rangers Administrator Hosannah Valentine, who helped me track down every storyteller. Mountain climber, firefighter, writer, innovator — Hosannah set up almost every interview. Her love for IDPs and refugees radiates in her training of Burma teens to become Junior Free Burma Rangers!

And also, to multi-talented Micah Beckwith, who

FROM THE WRITER

assisted me with interviews. Micah helps train Rangers in one of the most dangerous regions in Burma. With his missionary heritage, his grasp of languages and cultures helped me immensely.

Richard Drebert
www.richarddrebert.com

INTRODUCTION

A woman in Kachin State, Burma, kneels at a stream *listening* after an explosion. She prays that a pangolin (anteater) triggered a landmine. Or perhaps a mortar malfunctioned somewhere. But the next detonation seems nearer. If a machine gun chatters or rifle fire echoes close by — it's time to gather the children and *run*.

In this book, seven Free Burma Rangers — soldiers, guerrilla fighters, a mother, teachers and medics — reveal their personal stories.

Like hundreds of Rangers now serving in jungle communities of Burma (Myanmar), our storytellers wandered paths mined with discouragement before finding purpose with the Free Burma Rangers. Now, a compelling inner voice guides them on every challenging trail.

Rangers have died in Burma — from bullets, from drowning in river crossings, from jungle fevers and lightning strikes — but heartaches only burnish brighter the Rangers' objectives:

To bring help, hope and love to people of all faiths and ethnicities in the conflict zones of Burma, to shine a light on the actions of oppressors, to stand with the oppressed and support leaders and organizations committed to liberty, justice and service.

RANGERS IN THE GAP

Karen Eubank (co-founder, Free Burma Rangers) *listens.*

Her children, Sahale, 13, Suuzanne, 11, and Peter, 7, awaken as their father, Dave Eubank (founder, Free Burma Rangers), rouses them out of warm sleeping bags.

In the south of Burma, IDPs (internally displaced people) live under conditional cease-fire agreements. In the south, Free Burma Rangers help IDPs rebuild communities, establish schools and build medical clinics.

But in the Kachin State, a region near the China border, the Eubanks must *stay alert to stay alive.*

Rice for breakfast. Then, Dave, Karen and the kids hit the trail to find a Kachin IDP hide site. Kachin Independence Army guerrillas take point, and Dave drops behind his wife and kids, watchful. It's a family hike with *purpose.* Karen and Dave carry heavy rucksacks full of medical supplies.

To the hundreds of wounded and sick Kachin IDPs, antibiotics are valued above rubies and jade.

Kachin independence fighters have agreed to a truce, but MI-24 attack helicopters continue to fire rockets at camps. Burma Air Force jets strafe villagers, thought to be resistance supporters. Tatmadaw (Burma Army) troops burn rice fields and kill every pig, chicken and dog.

Here in the Kachin State, thundering rotors and the screams of jet turbines terrify children.

The Burma Army is pouring new foundations for commercial enterprise — mixed with the blood of its own people.

INTRODUCTION

The Eubanks have been helping families in Asia since long before Dave was a Special Forces soldier and Karen a special ed schoolteacher. In the '60s, Dave Eubank's father and mother were missionaries and broke trail with elephant pack trains.

Today, under the leadership of Dave and Karen, the Free Burma Rangers have completed 900 relief missions. Each year, 71 trained teams, of mostly ethnic Burmese, bring help, hope and love to thousands of homeless families subsisting in jungle and mountain camps throughout Burma.

Eight of these FBR teams are conducting relief missions in the Kachin State today, and Rangers are presently training more Kachin relief workers at hidden camps.

Like the seven Free Burma Rangers in our stories, Sahale, Suuzanne and Peter Eubank are traveling their own paths to know God's purpose for their lives. Together, the Eubank family prayerfully stays zeroed in on God's sovereign will, and they *thrive* — whether scaling Mount Rainier, hunting on the Alaska tundra with friends while on furlough or hiking in a Kachin State war zone.

They serve with an international family of Free Burma Rangers and follow one leader: *Jesus.*

It is their sincere hope that these stories motivate friends and neighbors to help the Free Burma Rangers deliver relief to the one million displaced people of Burma.

Richard Drebert

CHAPTER 1
COMMANDER'S INTENT
DAVE EUBANK'S STORY

*"We will always stand with the oppressed.
Not because we are so brave, but because it is right."*
Dave Eubank — Founder, Free Burma Rangers
(Speaking to a Tatmadaw Officer)

Warrior Born

Helplessly, I watched my squad of paratroopers bouncing across Georgia hardpan like rag dolls.

I drifted above my fellow U.S. Army Rangers swinging like a plumb bob, yanking and finessing my own parachute risers (controls), while treetops lashed the air in a 30-mile-per-hour crosswind.

I weighed 145 pounds, and even with my M-16 and 70-pound combat load, the wind gusts slung me in wide, uncontrollable arcs.

RIP.

The acronym might easily correspond with my final jump in the Rangers Indoctrination Program. A tech had misread the anemometer (wind-speed gauge), and I was the last Ranger out of the C-130 troop door before a red light warned our jumpmaster to terminate the exercise.

RANGERS IN THE GAP

All five paratroopers below me now lay like crushed insects, chutes flapping in unruly surrender.

Landing flat-backed would stun me unconscious. It was likely that my chute would drag me, flaying my body on rocks and brush until some gnarled sapling impaled me.

A few feet above the earth I yanked one capewell (canopy release) on my chest to deflate half my parachute — but a crosswind gathered up every thread of silk, anyway. My flailing chute dragged me the distance of a football field until I jerked the other capewell and freed myself.

I lay on my back, stunned for a while, then gained hands and knees. My rodeo ride had ground my leather jump boots to shreds. Ammo, grenades, canteen and rifle were torn from my ruck, and Fort Benning grit had buffed my helmet to a bright sheen.

Two of my squad lay tangled in a wire fence, and three others rested in heaps of fluttering silk.

Suddenly the wind died to a zephyr. I was about to roll free of my fouled lines when a commanding inner voice overpowered my sensory forces, and I tuned in to *Someone* speaking quietly, yet cryptically — as when a father kneels before a child, eye to eye.

It's not your time, David.

I recognized the voice. I hadn't heard it so plainly in years. I rubbed blood from my eyes and hollered at the nearest injured Rangers, but no one answered. Soon medics arrived to bear away the wounded.

I was the only Ranger who walked away from our macabre drop zone.

While recuperating in my bunk, a scene in Thailand played in my mind — one that I had nearly forgotten. In it, I stood in my yard holding an open pocketknife, declaring to the world: "I'm gonna be a soldier! And then I'm gonna be a missionary!"

I smiled at my childish oracle. Lt. David Eubank would never be a missionary like his gentle, compassionate father.

I was born to be a warrior.

Sam Yaek

I clung like a hairless white monkey atop my wooden swing set, screaming at a scrawny, pointy-eared dog. The hound leaped for me, snapping at my dangling bare feet, and I felt myself slipping.

"DAAAD!"

Suddenly a black-and-gray cloud of dust swallowed up the red dog.

Duke, my German Shepherd, clamped the hound's throat in iron jaws, shook him unconscious, then pinned him to the dirt until he stopped breathing. Duke was my protector, patrolling the yard for snakes, and warning our family when anyone approached our home that was situated close to the Thai-Burma border.

I dropped to the ground and hugged my hero, my 5-year-old heart still beating in my ears. Duke sniffed the hound warily. It jerked a bit, and I ran to the house to find Mom or Dad.

But Duke paid a price to rescue his boy. Red flecks drizzled down his fur where the rabid dog's teeth had nicked his shoulder. My family hoped that Duke might survive, but rabies symptoms developed quickly.

I experienced a sad *Old Yeller* day in Thailand. Losing Duke was my first lesson in what Mom called "suffering." She was my schoolteacher, and the Bible was my primer.

My 3-year-old sister, Ruth, my 2-year-old sister, Laurie, my dad, my mom and I lived in a two-story *Little House on the Prairie* home, about a day's muddy or dusty drive from Bangkok.

Missionaries Allan and Joan Eubank (Dad and Mom) had moved to the edge of the Thai jungle in 1961, just nine months after I was born.

Dad had been a Texas oilman and my mom a performer in Hollywood and Broadway before they answered God's call to be missionaries in Thailand.

My mother, Joan Hovis, had been singing with a USO troupe in Korea when she captivated my father with her beauty and Christian character. After sharing a cozy candlelight dinner and a single kiss, they sailed for contrasting destinies — though neither forgot their deeply spiritual connection.

Dad often received letters from London, Hollywood or New York, but he was resigned that Mom's dream was to become a star with her name in Broadway lights.

After Dad served out his Army commission, a sharply

chiseled command from God blindsided him. Allan felt called to "be a missionary."

"Lord, I'm willing. But let me make a million dollars in the oil business — then I can go all out for you!"

College trained as an engineer and geologist, Allan Eubank worked for oil companies in Texas for a few years. He drilled ambitiously, but never felt God's endorsement on his plan to be a rich philanthropist. Dad tossed his dreams of wealth to the Texas winds and chose to follow Jesus *without* qualification. He entered Brite Divinity School at Texas Christian University in Fort Worth, Texas, to prepare for missions work in Thailand.

"I was 28 years old and finally knew why I was born," Dad writes in his book *God! If You Are Really God!*

Then, in my father's third year at Brite seminary, Broadway star Joan Hovis danced into his life again. She "happened" to be performing at the Casa Mañana Theater, a mile away from where he lived. She starred in the musical *Oklahoma!*

Mom had been chosen for a Theatre World Award as one of the 10 most "Promising Personalities" on Broadway. But more than anything else, my mother wanted to serve God fully.

When she felt God speaking very plainly to her, "No one can serve two masters, Joan," my mother knew she needed to make some life-altering choices.

In her season of renewed commitment to Jesus, Dad began attending her performances at the Casa Mañana — and within weeks he won her heart.

Mom finished up her road shows with renowned playwright and composer Richard Rodgers (of Rodgers and Hammerstein) to become a bride and missionary.

In 1959, Dad discovered the gusher he had always hoped for: Mom joined him in the adventure of a lifetime! With actors, soldiers and oilmen in attendance, Allan Eubank and Joan Hovis became husband and wife. After mission studies, in 1961, Dad and Mom were ordained as ministers with the Christian Church Disciples of Christ.

Circling over Bangkok rice paddies, my father took my mother's hand and said, "I feel like we're coming home."

Mom smiled down at me in her arms and replied, "That's exactly how I feel, too."

At a village called Sam Yaek, about 50 miles west of Bangkok, my parents settled down to help plant churches in Thailand. Our first home was nestled in a valley of rice paddies, where years earlier, farmers had carved fields from lush forests of teak and bamboo. Sam Yaek served as my childhood FOB (forward operating base), and the miles of agricultural land became my "big game" hunting grounds.

"Look what I got, Mom!"

Exciting creatures crawled and flew everywhere, like centipedes longer than hotdogs, spiders with legs the length of my forearm and beetles that bounced off rafters like baseballs. Chickens, dogs, pigs and cattle scurried and wandered along worn footpaths, sleeping under the bamboo houses at night.

COMMANDER'S INTENT

Villagers' homes around us were constructed with woven bamboo walls set solidly upon teak posts. To guard against flooding in the rainy season, each two- or three-room house perched about 6 feet or more off the ground. A set of teak ladder-stairs welcomed sandals or bare feet, and above it all, a family slept under a roof of thatch, palm fronds or tin.

Only one of Thailand's local denizens sent shivers up my boyhood spine. Bats flew into my loft bedroom from an opening in the roof. I recall their scrabbling claws on the ceiling and their flapping "capes." I spent restless nights worrying that they might drain my blood while I slept.

Although my family appeared typically American with conveniences like plumbing, the Eubanks' hearts grew more Asian year by year. Dad and Mom immersed themselves in our neighbors' culture and, for my sisters and me, English became our second language *after* Thai.

Along with schooling us kids, Mom included the local women and children in the chores and the challenges of her daily life. Her trained voice had serenaded thousands in Europe and the United States, but now she sang at humble gatherings of villagers, teaching them hymns like "What a Friend We Have in Jesus."

Dad mentored me in the traditions of his father, a Christian man of integrity, a veteran of World War I and a Texan through and through. Grandpa taught Dad to shoot a .22 rifle before he was 6 years old, and I hunted lizards, snakes and squirrels at a young age as well.

I learned to swim like a jungle perch, and Dad nurtured my adventure cravings — Mom juggled evangelism work, keeping up with wash, dinners and chores, *plus* homeschooling a boy who daydreamed of killing tigers. Finally, my parents decided that I needed a structured academic environment.

Make-believe commando patrols at Sam Yaek ended when I was 7 years old. Dad and Mom enrolled me at the Chiang Mai Coeducational Center (CCC — later called the Chiang Mai International School), and loneliness for my family nearly broke my heart.

Jungle Boy in the City

Seeing Dad's wide smile and feeling his bear hug at CCC hurt worse now than waving from my train seat two months earlier.

I lay on a sweaty double bed with my father, staring at his thick chest rising and falling in the half light. Dad wasn't sleeping, either. He had driven to Bangkok and flown hundreds of miles to attend a meeting and see how I fared at boarding school.

My new home housed 27 students whose fathers were diplomats, oil company employees, missionaries and military liaisons.

The school building had been headquarters for the Japanese 7th Cavalry (an occupying force during World War II), and my first weeks at CCC were as close to torture as I could have imagined. I had buried my face in a thin pillow to keep anyone from hearing me cry myself to sleep.

Then came the dengue fever. My temperature climbed to 104 degrees, while inside my skull something hammered and poked until I vomited up *nothing* again and again for days. A nurse checked on me periodically, but most of the time I lay alone in my bunk while classes were in session.

This was the first time in my short life that I turned to God in desperate need. Shivering in afternoon sweats, I whispered to Jesus, "Mom and Dad believe in you, but they aren't here to pray. So, Jesus, if you're real, help me."

The moment I said "Jesus," a heavy cloud seemed to lift, and the room grew brighter. From outside of me, *Someone* embraced my sweaty body. His arms felt comforting, like my mother's, and suddenly I realized that I wasn't alone. God, whom my dad preached about and my mom sang about, was REAL.

I recovered my strength and began adjusting to living separate from my parents and sisters — when Dad showed up.

Lying with my father, homesickness reclaimed me, like the final act in a tragic play. I scooted against Dad and lay my head on his chest, weeping, missing my childhood in Sam Yaek. Dad came close to bundling me up and taking me home to my mom. But amid my grief and my father's empathy, God was engraving a detailed map upon our souls for his specific purposes.

For eight years, Mom and Dad had journeyed by foot, and sometimes with an elephant pack train, preaching to remote tribes. They helped build churches, schools and handcraft co-ops and established prayer groups in villages.

Among ethnic tribes, the Eubank integrity and social standing blazed a trail for thousands of bold missionary and relief workers in years to come. And living in boarding schools at a young age tempered me for the mental and physical demands of my own unique calling.

At CCC, it took weeks, but my acute loneliness began to subside. During Thanksgiving break, my parents scraped together the price of a ticket to fly me home to Sam Yaek.

With my family and friends, Dad baptized me, affirming my trust in Jesus Christ, who promised never to forsake me.

In 1971, when I was 11, Mom and Dad, Ruth, 9, Laurie, 8, and my new baby sister, Suewannee, 2, moved to Chiang Mai, where Dad took a position at Payap University teaching New Testament and evangelism. Mom taught music and drama, and the six of us Eubanks were reunited!

I galloped my horse across acres of rice fields or climbed mountain passes around Doi Suthep, a few miles from our home. We filled up a whole restless, happy pew at our Chiang Mai church, and I couldn't get enough of *family*. Boy Scout camping, Mom's scrumptious dinners — and keeping pace with Dad as he visited churches in the hill country.

COMMANDER'S INTENT

In Chiang Mai, as in Sam Yaek, the centerpiece of our social lives continued to be a weekly prayer meeting taking place in our living room. Neighbors gathered to petition God for healing sick people. Men or women troubled by evil spirits often asked my parents and their friends to help free them from demons, and my sisters and I often witnessed unexplainable supernatural events in the company of my father and mother.

At every opportunity, when Dad wasn't teaching at the university, he led groups at a blazing pace into the mountains to evangelize in villages. Dad was at war with the unseen world bent upon ruining the souls of men and women — but as a missionary kid, I shrugged off my powerful Christian heritage.

ॐॐॐ

By my last year at CCC, academics and sports only whetted my appetite for greater challenges, and one day an adversary showed up at school who was carved from the same Thai hardwood as I.

"I hear you think you're tough, Eubank ..." Pete Dawson smirked.

I was, but I was also a lightweight, so I always resorted to the same tactic on beefy opponents: shock and speed. Strike first — *hard.*

A fight with this new eighth-grader from the States was inevitable (students had been egging us on all day). I figured he would go down with my first strikes, and I could be on his neck with a chokehold in seconds. He would either give up or pass out.

At 14, I was the undisputed stud in my school, and there were several guys who would relish me getting thrashed unconscious. But I'd die before I let that happen. Pete was a wrestler and quarterback — and annoyingly good at talking smack.

I would enjoy this one …

I didn't answer Pete. I jammed my fist into his throat, and he hunched a bit as I slid behind him like a python. I hugged him to my chest, my arm squeezing against his windpipe. My power came from 20 pull-ups a day, so in cranking his thick neck, I expected him to drop to his knees, and he did.

But somehow he stood up again — with me hanging off his back. No one I ever fought survived my wiry-armed chokehold. Suddenly he lunged backward, slamming me against walls and concrete pillars, trying to break my hold — or my spine.

Pete introduced my head to every sharp edge in the room as his face grew red as betel nut juice, but he wouldn't give up! I figured if I could just hold on long enough … but I was interrupted. A few skinny teachers and a burly PE coach pried my locked arms loose.

After the usual scoldings and threats from teachers, Pete and I shook hands with iron grips.

You know, I think I like this guy …

And Pete was thinking the same thing. During our last year before graduating from CCC, Pete and I spent most of our free time in mock battles before or after school and on weekends. Our fights cinched a lifelong friendship (and paved the way for Pete to marry my sister Laurie).

When I left for my new boarding school, I was a sturdy 15 year old, about 5 feet, 8 inches, known around Chiang Mai as the farang (white boy) with a rifle. I said a respectful farewell to prayer meetings and church, ready to challenge the world with mind and fists at the International School of Bangkok (ISB).

Even the potheads worked hard to get good grades at my new boarding school. Airline CEOs, generals, ambassadors and diplomats sent their kids to the ISB, expecting sons and daughters to excel later at prestigious universities back in the States.

But at ISB, Pete Dawson and I grew tired of our bloodless battles. In our spare time we mixed with Thai gangs and challenged other young men from school to brawl on Bangkok street corners.

The local thugs were surprised that I spoke their language like a native-born Thai. And at the end of every successful fight, I locked in my memory the most effective, painful moves that weakened and defeated an opponent.

I excelled in sports, too, like basketball, but a love of fighting churned in my soul like Salween River rapids. No sport came close to the challenge and thrill of hand-to-hand combat. As a teenager, I learned that if I never gave up, no matter how bloody or beaten, I most often won in the end.

RANGERS IN THE GAP

Wounded Soldier

Confession is good for the soul ...

I sat slumped on Mom's sofa, head hanging like a dejected puppy. I had told Dad everything: my drinking Mekong sours (whiskey) with other farangs at Pop's Bar in Bangkok; my most recent altercations; skipping church; even my intentional fouls playing Singapore in the Thailand National Basketball Championship (we won).

"Let's pray about it, David."

Challenging myself at school or on the streets stole every waking moment and my dreams, too. I spoke to God seldom as a teenager, except when I went to church, but talking over my failings with Dad always seemed the next best thing to prayer when I came home on holidays.

I graduated when I was 18 and decamped to the States with a full ROTC scholarship. I enrolled at Texas A&M University, the same college where my granddad and father received their degrees in engineering.

Since high school, the ambition of leading men in combat had seized my heart, and my university instructors set my flight path toward an Army commission. I lived like a warrior monk, ignoring distractions like girls or parties. During college, I discovered mountain climbing, snow skiing, hunting and distance running. I spun on a breathtaking axis of adventure, with a long-term objective: to wear the green beret of Army Special Forces.

But in my early 20s, on the way to visit my family in Chiang Mai, a question came out of nowhere, like an RPG (rocket-propelled grenade): *Will God destroy my map for the future?*

Officers had marked me for leadership and chosen me for Army Airborne School. I already wore paratroopers' wings in my third year of cadet training. But I knew the stories: God had turned my parents' destinies upside down. I worried about new orders that Jesus might give me.

Mom and Dad's prayer meetings started out as humdrum as I remembered, but out of respect I didn't flop on my bed upstairs like I had as a teenager. Instead, I reached deeply for some spiritual maturity — hoping to interact meaningfully with the powerhouse Christians who gathered here.

While mumbling along with the songs, some unsettling thoughts invaded my mind: *I've never asked if it was God's will that I become a soldier. Have I screwed up?*

"Is there anyone here who would like prayer about the future?"

Ian Talbot was a British missionary and pastor who worked with my parents, and I had known him all my life. I held my breath and lifted my hand.

Reverend Talbot placed his big hands on my shoulders — and gradually a flood of *something* enveloped me, like electricity reaching down to my toes.

I had *heard* about this kind of super-spiritual stuff, and I prayed — truly humbled.

"Lord, I'm so sorry that I didn't talk to you about what

I should do. I took the ROTC scholarship because I wanted to be in the Army ..."

God had been patient with me. He had allowed me to experience Army life, at least until *now.*

"Thank you for letting me be a paratrooper! But I give all that up for you, if that's what you want. I'll go to Africa as a missionary or *wherever* you say ..."

Reverend Talbot's voice broke through my whispered prayers, and I knew that God was speaking through him directly to me. I expected God to say that I was forgiven but to trade in my military books for a Bible. But that's not what God said.

"Keep doing what I have called you to do. I'm preparing you for service. You will face an event that will almost break you, but don't be afraid — it will not crush you. And, Dave, you'll always *know* when I'm speaking to you."

Nothing so "spiritual" had ever happened to me before. I came away from the Chiang Mai prayer meeting sensing my Commander's Intent (his overall purpose) and believing that God would unfold my destiny, mission by mission.

I graduated from Texas A&M and U.S. Army Ranger School as a second lieutenant.

I entered the Officer Basic Course at Fort Benning, training in tactics, mechanized warfare, aircraft control, weapons systems, communications, heavy weaponry, maps and compass, artillery, maneuvering forces, offensive and defensive movement and war games.

COMMANDER'S INTENT

I wondered how God could ever use war craft in serving him — but I marched on his last orders. Fresh out of training, the Army shipped me to Panama, where I led a platoon of 40 men — my first command. I was 23.

In the Army infantry, extreme feats of strength and endurance get a soldier noticed, and I credit Mom's DNA from Granddad Hovis for my promotion to scout platoon leader.

In 1929, my granddad, Freeman Hovis, was a short, wiry "strongman" and a popular showman who toured the South as a bare-knuckle boxer, rodeo clown and singer.

My grandmother, Ruth, was a 17-year-old beauty who lived on a Mississippi farm. Ruth had just graduated from high school when my granddad, a charmer, came calling.

They eloped, and Freeman swept Ruth into a cross-country adventure. He performed in rodeos and sideshows before settling in Washington State and finally Texas. Ruth had two sons and a daughter with the strongman: Larry became a writer and movie producer, acting in the hit comedy series *Hogan's Heroes*. Michael became a movie producer as well.

But Freeman's daughter, Joan (my mother), was the star of Freeman's heart long before she was a stage sensation. The showman recognized talent in his adolescent daughter and drove her to perfection in dance and to near-perfect pitch in her singing. (To this day, Mom credits Granddad Hovis for her love of professionalism in the arts.)

I never met Granddad, but his legacy of endurance and

his demand for excellence in all endeavors flows in my veins — as well as his love for all things *risky.*

In Panama, in a 12-mile road competition, I carried a 40-pound rucksack in abhorrent Canal Zone humidity, breaking all records for speed — and my battalion commander noticed. Then I won the multinational Panama Stud Man Triathlon — and the commander called me to his office.

"Eubank, I want you to take over as reconnaissance commander for the battalion. You're our eyes and ears now."

Leading a battalion scout platoon, I applied my own unique strategies in jungle recon and felt the same thrill as street fighting in Bangkok. My hand-picked team dropped inside hot zones to map terrain, measure armed resistance or train local troops in guerrilla warfare.

అఛఛఛ

As an Army infantry commander, I had deployed with my platoon deep into the Peruvian jungle to recon and photograph major narcotics operations. Our extraction had been delayed, and my soldiers slumped against the vibrating fuselage in a C-130 examining toe blisters and dreaming about a bath after a month in the swamps.

But I held a penlight in my teeth, studying a topo map, plotting the next mountain I would summit. I glanced at my men, and no one met my eyes. They knew what I was thinking. They had more pressing engagements than rock climbing the first week back after a hard mission.

My mind tracked off the map for a moment as I thought about a young woman I had begun dating. Trish lived up to my officer's demand for visual excellence, and she seemed to embrace my Christian ideals. Admittedly, I was green as grass when it came to women. I romanced Trish like conquering a gendarme (mountain spire), ignoring every warning in the Bible about unequal relationships. After a short-range courtship, we tied the knot, and as in all marriages, the real Dave and Trish suddenly showed up. Trish struggled to meet my unrealistic demands, and it irritated me that our union was only a caricature of what my parents enjoyed.

I.expected my wife to match my blistering pace in life, and she fell farther and farther behind. Our tempestuous union lasted only three years.

Moments after our divorce was final, I felt relieved because now I could pursue Special Forces action, unhindered.

I followed Trish out of the courthouse after signing the papers — and suddenly she stopped.

She said, "Dave, I'm so angry at you."

Dumb grunt that I am, I was shocked. "Why are you mad at me?"

Tears welled up in Trish's eyes. "You were not supposed to *let* me divorce you."

An avalanche of remorse buried me as I watched her walk away. I had failed to rescue Trish when she was falling.

Alone in my apartment, the weight of my folly pressed me to my knees.

"Jesus, what have I done? Oh, God ..."

Guilt beat me to an emotional pulp. I sobbed like a 7-year-old boy again, then took stock of my position: I had hauled a godless 50-caliber attitude into my marriage, and the knowledge of my shortcomings had arrived too late to rescue our relationship.

Even worse: *I had wrecked the integrity of my Eubank name.*

I made a new promise to consult Jesus in every decision I made, assuming that prowling jungles in war paint was all I would ever be tasked to do thereafter.

Burma in Brief

The year after my parents and I arrived in Thailand, our neighbors in Burma (now called Myanmar) faced political upheavals that impacted people on both sides of the Thai-Burma boundary line.

During the '60s, while Allan and Joan Eubank sometimes traveled by pachyderm preaching about a God of peace, a new socialist dictatorship plundered the sovereignty of rice farmers and villagers in Burma. Resistance groups sprouted like bamboo shoots and cobbled together machetes and castoff World War II rifles to defend themselves.

A communist general named Ne Win launched a campaign called The Four Cuts, designed to sever supply lines (food, funds, information and recruits) to guerrilla groups who opposed his Army, known as the Tatmadaw. Ne Win's Tatmadaw officers built permanent jungle camps from which his battalions terrorized families suspected of helping resistance fighters. Villages were systematically ransacked, then burned, the citizens enslaved for work projects.

After Ne Win, the Tatmadaw (Burma Army) steadily gained power under succeeding military generals. Tatmadaw tentacles reached into nearly every state in Burma, giving rise to more and more ragtag resistance armies, some as different in cultures as the monsoon and dry seasons.

In 1988, after quelling a democracy movement including Buddhist monks, college students, farmers and businessmen, the wealthy generals retrofitted their dictatorship, calling themselves the State Law and Order Restoration Council (SLORC).

They celebrated their power by renaming the entire nation "Myanmar." Ethnics in the resistance movements reject the new name, even to this day, refusing to wear the dictators' brand.

During the '88 democracy crusade, a few amateur journalists outflanked the junta, exposing the murders of thousands of protesters. And though major television networks were intrigued by dead bodies for a time, media spotlights never really penetrated the jungle warrens where orphans and uprooted families hid like animals from the Tatmadaw.

RANGERS IN THE GAP

In the '90s, the SLORC launched a fresh campaign of terror, burning villages and torturing headmen (mayors). Tatmadaw officers ordered homeowners to relocate to military-controlled settlements — bearing only what personal items a family could carry in a single trip.

A new day was dawning in Burma. Outside interests salivated over Myanmar's oil and natural gas wealth. Mining companies negotiated with the SLORC for rights to extract precious metals, gems and minerals. Burma Army battalions guarded foreign engineers who built dams to power industry — displacing farmers who had harvested rice there for generations.

China supplied armaments and training for Tatmadaw ground forces that grew to 400,000 strong. An appetite for heroin (chemically processed opium) in Asia and the West set Burma on course to be number two in global poppy production. Opium farmers harvested multiple tons of poppies in the remote Wa region (an area carved from Northeastern Shan State), along the China-Burma border.

The Wa government created its own armed force: the United Wa State Army (UWSA) to guard the sovereignty of their new Wa State. The UWSA negotiated a cease-fire with the Tatmadaw by paying tribute with opium and heroin.

As recently as 1979, Wa tribesmen had been offering demon spirits human sacrifices and performing latou (headhunting). At the same time, Wa Christians (descendents of converts of British missionaries) were building churches and seeing Wa hearts changed.

Only opium production propped up the frail Wa economy — and Wa Christians spoke out about the ruinous effects that narcotics had upon their society. Christians paid for their crusade with blood and imprisonment by secret police, but still they gained seats in the Wa government.

In 1993, the Wa State Foreign Ministry asked the United Nations for agricultural help to wean them off opium dependency. They planned to replace opium with crops like rubber, rice and tea. They also asked the United States to protect them from the Tatmadaw while they made the unpopular transition.

But to those in the region, it seemed the UN ignored their desperate pleas. And despite imposing an economic embargo, the U.S. government did not otherwise publicly get involved. The Wa delegation in Thailand informed Christian leaders in Chiang Mai about the rebuff and advised Wa ethnic leader U Saw Lu to speak to Pastor Allan Eubank.

By praying together in Dad's living room at Chiang Mai, my father and U Saw Lu shared in God's blueprint to bond a Special Forces officer and a special education teacher, who forged an alliance of love that would touch a nation.

Romantic Odyssey

Uncle Sam had assigned me to command joint exercises with the Thai Special Forces — and I was *home.*

My altimeter read 20,000 feet as I leaped from a cargo door above our drop zone. I breathed oxygen through my HALO (High Altitude Low Opening) helmet, as well as a quick prayer for the Thai commandos I had been training.

In 1990, I had graduated from the Special Forces Qualification Course in the States, then followed up with elite forces training in survival and evasion tactics, resistance and escape and terrorism awareness. I also completed the Command Language Program and, later, the Command and General Staff College Program.

From a few thousand feet above my Thai team, I unfastened my oxygen mask and watched my trainees. Each soldier had reached terminal velocity and soared for several minutes before opening and navigating canopies for gentle landings in a designated rice field. I circled above them, an eagle guarding fledglings, enjoying the agrarian view: green fields, villages, grazing water buffalo and farmers easing their backs as they waved.

High altitude parachute drops fed my hunger for adventure, and teaching Thai commandos the art of soaring under radar (in my backyard!) was a blessing straight from God.

Yet, even so, during this primo duty assignment, I struggled with God's direction for my life. I loved my work as a captain, commanding two A teams: one special reconnaissance detachment *and* my HALO detachment. Our missions were classified and high priority — but I couldn't shake the feeling that jumping out of planes and tracking down bad guys wasn't my purpose for living.

Humbled by my divorce and locked on stand down while the military mopped up after the short Gulf War, I returned to Washington State with two objectives: to serve a stint in the Middle East before the war was history and determine *exactly* God's will for my life.

And should I dial back my gung-ho intensity before looking for a relationship with a woman again? One thing I knew: Any woman I dated would be as sold out to Jesus as I was.

Erica was just such a young woman. I had known her since childhood, but after one ill-fated Yosemite trip, she decided that we weren't a good match.

She let me down easy. "But I know a girl who might actually *enjoy* this, Dave. You need to meet Karen. I'll introduce you ..."

When Erica pointed me out to Karen Huesby, I had already been studying Karen during the church service like a book on a high shelf. I was still a little untrained in the rules of engagement, so I waited for a proper introduction.

"So. You're in the Army?" Karen asked me as Erica sauntered away with a self-satisfied look.

I suddenly floated above verdant fields at rice harvest. Karen's hazel eyes were captivating.

"Actually, I'm in the Special Forces," I managed to say.

I waited, but the words made no impression — she'd never heard of it.

"I'm a Green Beret. You know ..."

Her polite headshake and smile said: *Nope. I don't.*

"Were you in the Gulf War?" she asked.

I changed tactics. "No, I was too scared ..." Now *that* was a joke, and surely she would get it.

"You know. It's really *okay* to be scared."

It seldom happened, but I was speechless. The girl was dead serious!

We spent the evening with friends whom we both knew, and when I had interrogated her enough to discover that she was a devout Christian, I asked to see her again for dinner.

Not a chance, soldier.

She didn't say it that way, but I got the message.

Our odyssey of hearts might have ended that late evening, but I followed up with an invitation that piqued her curiosity. She had graduated from Seattle Pacific University, targeting a job as a special ed teacher, and she was growing to love the outdoors. I happened to be planning a technical ascent of Mount Shuksan in the Northern Cascades.

"You can stay at the base camp with friends while I do the hard stuff, or you can climb with us right to the top. Your choice."

"Can I bring a friend?"

I agreed, and six of us ended up preparing dinner and heading up the mountain at midnight when the ice was firm. It turned out to be a historic climb — for me. Three climbers quit after several hundred feet of using ice axes.

"You game?" I asked Karen. We stared up at a steep

wall of ice luring *me* to the summit. But what was Karen thinking? Her red face was beaming.

I snapped a climbing rope to the 100-pound blonde and started up, placing ice screws along the route and fastening her line to each one as protection from a slip. Karen emulated my moves, jamming crampons deep into the cold mountain face, until I paused to rest before the last push to the top. Before this final vertical climb I figured I should take stock of her mental state — it wouldn't be getting any easier, and we had a long descent to consider.

I stared down between my knees.

"So, how're you doing, Karen?"

Joy in her face lit up the whole mountain as she replied, "I'm diggin' this!"

I just shook my head. She seemed relaxed on her first technical ascent, like it was her 20th!

On our descent to base camp, I grew reflective. I told Jesus, "I'll do anything, Lord, if I can marry this woman."

But romance wasn't on Karen's mind — especially with a muscle-bound type like me. Karen had never dated before. She was probably waiting for a spiritual, patient, well-bred urban dweller to fall madly in love with her someday. Our personalities were so *different*.

I never sauntered anywhere, but marched — even in Walmart — always ordered by some inner mission. I was eight years older than Karen and on a rebound after a divorce. I could be opinionated and intense, but I was learning to be quiet and listen to a woman's heart.

A man like me might threaten her objectives and confuse her emotions if she let him into her world. At least that's what she thought *before* God answered my prayers.

We never called it dating, but our relationship included hours of mountain climbing, skiing and long walks in the Washington forests. We started out inviting people to accompany us, but I whittled down our number of "chaperones," little by little.

As trust grew stronger, I poured out my heart to Karen, explaining the details of my mistakes with Trish. I bared my soul concerning my inner battle about remaining in the military. I explained how inadequate and tainted I felt when I considered pursuing Christian service.

Karen nurtured my desire to follow Jesus by listening, and without her, I might never have realized God's plan for my future.

As sudden as a flash flood, one day I decided to end my military career. I yearned for the satisfaction I saw in my father's eyes — a fulfillment never gained from my most daring Special Forces mission.

At 32 years old, I leaped into the dark to find my purpose for being alive — and I wanted Karen to go with me.

I applied to Fuller Theological Seminary in Pasadena, California, at the same time telling Karen that she was the one I believed God wanted me to marry.

But *my* adventure wasn't hers. She had achieved her lifelong dream to serve children as a special ed teacher in Seattle. God was using her gifts of patience, love and unshakeable devotion to help students with learning disabilities succeed.

My Eubank intensity frightened Karen, and she needed space to think about the whole situation.

"We need to stop seeing each other, Dave."

The heartbreak drove me to my knees. "Lord, if you want me to go to the mission field somewhere as a single man, I will," I prayed, but I hoped Karen would change her mind.

Months passed, and we spent time together at Christmas. I asked if we might start over. She said no.

I loved my Biblical studies in my first year at Fuller, but looked forward to spring break when I hoped to jumpstart Karen's interest. But during my visit to Seattle, I couldn't ignite a single positive spark.

Finally, I offered to chauffeur her to Los Angeles to see family, since it was on my way back to Fuller. She accepted the offer and busily packed her suitcases. We had one hour left before our drive. Soon Karen might ignore me for hundreds of miles with her nose in a book.

I wasn't going to waste a second of critical alone time.

I told her roommate, "I don't care who calls, I don't want to be disturbed …" Then I reconsidered. "The only person I'll talk to is my father …"

Dad never called me unless it was an emergency.

I took a deep breath and prayed one more time silently that Karen would have a change of heart — and the telephone rang.

Burma Callings

"Dad?"

My father didn't dillydally. "Dave, U Saw Lu, who serves in the Wa Foreign Ministry, is visiting with me. He is here in Chiang Mai trying to get international support for a plan to transform the Wa economy. He wants the UN and our government to help them replace opium with crops like rubber and tea. They have refused, I'm afraid.

"He's asking for missionaries to come to the Wa State. He believes that only Jesus can change the hearts of the Wa.

"U Saw Lu noticed your picture on our wall — the one with your green beret. He asked if you were a Christian, and I explained that you were my son, studying at seminary. He asked if you would go to Burma and help the Wa people. I told Lu that we should pray about it, and we did — then we called you."

No mission from any commander ever gripped my soul with such authority. My answer can only be described as pure inner *worship*.

"Dad, how soon do they want me?"

I would be one of the first Western men to enter the Wa State in 30 years.

I hung up the phone.

"Karen, I need to talk to you ..." I poured out my heart one last time. "I want you to marry me and come to Burma. I understand if you don't want to, but I really need you. One way or another, I have to go."

"When will you come back?"

I tried to keep my excitement in check when I sensed a crack in Karen's resolve. She never made snap decisions, and we were both caught in an emotional freefall.

"Three months. I'll be back for the new semester at Fuller. But if God has other plans, I may *never* come back."

I might be a celibate, single, lonely missionary in the jungle, for God only knows how long.

Like a check on ammo before a firefight, I breathed my commitment one last time.

I barely remember a single mile of our drive through Washington, Oregon and California. A quiet thrill stirred our hearts, like when Karen and I stared up at a pristine peak before a climb. As we approached Carmel, I suggested that we rest at the home of a sniper friend. He wasn't at the house when we arrived, so we killed time walking on the beach — and suddenly *all* of Karen's heart spilled out for the first time.

Her words tasted so sweet to my soul: "Dave, I don't want you to leave me, and I don't want you to 'never' come back!"

"Well, you've told me what you don't want. Tell me what you do want, Karen."

"I want you to follow God, Dave."

"Do you want to marry me?"

"Yes, but … can you let me sleep on it?"

For the first time during our remarkable courtship, I knew that Karen was mine. God confirmed it to me on the white sands of Carmel by the sea. By morning, God had cleared any clouds of uncertainty in Karen's heart.

I finished out my semester at Fuller in Pasadena, and Karen resigned her position as teacher in Seattle. Three months later, on a beautiful beach, my mother's powerful voice echoed in the cliffs of Malibu singing "Let Me Be Your Servant." My father performed our June wedding ceremony, and we celebrated with friends and family — the same month that the Wa leaders expected us to arrive in Burma.

We honeymooned twice — once in Malibu, and again in Chiang Mai — before traveling by plane to the lawless Wa State in Northeastern Burma. After landing at an airfield, we hefted rucksacks loaded with medical supplies and Bible teaching material, then traveled by foot and 4x4 truck (if available) to remote Wa villages.

With the help of Wa leaders, we silently skirted battalions of the brutal Tatmadaw and camps of the unpredictable United Wa State Army soldiers.

For three months of each year, from 1993 to 1995, Karen and I lived with Christian, Buddhist, Communist and Animist villagers desperate for medical and economic relief.

After our three summer trips, we carried back the dream expressed by Christian Wa heads of state: They prayed for the moral and financial backing from the nations affected by the scourge of narcotics. That was more than 20 years ago, and the Wa people are still praying for help.

COMMANDER'S INTENT

And within this violent jungle frontier, the seeds of the Free Burma Rangers began to grow roots.

CHAPTER 2
DEFINING OUR MISSION
KAREN EUBANK'S STORY

In this new life I was attempting to lead, I cried out,
"What is my job description?"
And the answer surprised me: "Just be loving ..."
Karen Eubank — Co-founder, Free Burma Rangers

Rucksack University

When three scowling men emerged from the jungle shadows, Dave and I stopped dead.

Two of the renegade soldiers wore 3-foot-long "dhas" (swords) sheathed in bamboo scabbards, and one fingered a machete stuffed in his belt. I glanced at Dave, who smiled cordially and asked directions to Thao Mae village.

Machete Man's lips curled into a sly smile.

The men began speaking in low tones, staring at *me*, and Dave never glanced in my direction. Special Forces had trained him to mask his deadly side, but *I* knew what he was thinking. Machete Man would be the first soldier gasping for life in the mud if they made an aggressive move toward me.

But there were three of them ...

Machete Man tipped rainwater from his canvas hat brim, pointed to a trail — and suddenly all three could barely conceal the "joke." Likely their outpost lay along the path he indicated.

Lord Jesus, help us ...

For weeks, Dave and I had been sleeping in the jungle or with village families in the Wa State in Northeast Burma. We had been married a little more than a month, and wherever we traveled our white skin and bright-colored backpacks attracted stares like emergency flares.

Few Caucasians had journeyed through this region of Burma since World War II, when American and British troops joined ethnic tribes to drive the Japanese out. Only recently had Wa State authorities opened their borders to allow "tourists" to explore inside.

Dave and I had been slogging on muddy trails, as narrow as deer paths or as wide as logging roads, on our way to a destination where a plane would fly us back to our home in a neighboring country. We had been holding improvised Christian leadership classes, gaining rapport with village headmen and treating Wa villagers from our limited medical supplies and knowledge.

Suddenly Machete Man grasped my husband's wrist — and touched the handle of his weapon. His dark eyes met Dave's, expecting to cower the white tourist. I stood frozen to the mud while Machete Man's companions circled behind me. The sour smell of rice liquor hung in the air.

Dave spoke quietly in English, like I was a fellow soldier. "Karen, when I yell 'Go!' you dump your pack and *run.* Don't stop, no matter what's happening here. Run and don't look back."

And leave you alone?

As frightened as I was, I wasn't running anywhere.

෨෨෨

I wasn't interested in the Army guy I met at the First Presbyterian Church in Walla Walla. He seemed real sure of himself, and I dismissed him like I did most of the guys I had politely ignored since junior high. I was a good girl from the City of Angels, raised by devout Lutheran parents, and I had attended church regularly from the time I was in pigtails.

My dad had worked as manager for companies like Coca Cola, and at home he always finished Mom's honey-do lists shadowed by his curious little moppet. It was through working closely with my father that I learned to read the character of a man, and I had decided to reserve my heart for someone like Dad.

My mom excelled in her jobs as a homemaker and ICU nurse. Seeing her gifts in comforting hospitalized kids, dying patients and grieving families influenced me to pursue an academic path, serving children with my own gifts.

Maintaining A's in school was a challenge for me, but my little brother, David, struggled every minute to stay at his grade level. My confidence in teaching children later in life came from helping David prove everyone wrong and seeing him excel in his endeavors. Through my teens, I delighted in finding unorthodox but effective methods of helping him break through intellectual barriers.

ॐॐॐ

Cows! Haylofts and horses! Fresh peaches and cream before morning chores!

I lived a girl's country dream whenever I visited my cousins on their Walla Walla farm in Washington State. Dad had moved our family to a small house in the Walla Walla suburbs, when he partnered with relatives in a business installing commercial telephone systems. Mom resumed her profession in the ICU at a nearby hospital, and whenever I wasn't in school, I rode horses at the farm or practiced clarinet for marching band with my cousins.

While Dave was jumping out of C-130s, I was a skinny, bookish junior high student, living comfortably in my own quiet space.

In my teens, I opened the first page of my future marriage curriculum as I studied Mom and Dad, who endured financial upheavals that stretched their faith. Through their examples I learned that a family sticks together, even if emotional mortar shells burst all around them.

In Walla Walla, we settled upon the First Presbyterian Church for family worship, and it fit our fresh approach in serving God. I fell in love with the earnest, committed people at First Presbyterian — and especially with my new youth leaders who wore jeans and t-shirts to services. I found that experiencing God had little to do with appearance and *everything* to do with the sincerity of my heart.

When I became a teen leader in our Presbyterian youth group, I began to have questions about my family's traditional religion.

Am I taking a ride in my parents' hay wagon? What if the religion they taught me is not the right one? How do I really know?

I needed assurance that my relationship with Jesus was personal and genuine.

One Sunday morning at church, a diorama in my mind distracted me from our pastor's sermon as I pondered my destiny. I thought about my future children — and *their* children and beyond. I asked myself, *What's at the end of it all?*

Sunshine streamed from stained-glass panes touching everyone with lovely hues of light, and I realized that my choices colored everyone around me, too. If I believed that heaven waited for me at the end of it all, then my present faith in God would adorn the lives of people around me — like my parents' faith steadied and influenced me.

I must choose my way now. One path led to creativity and deep satisfaction. The other led to emptiness. In this reflective moment as I sat in the pew, Jesus splashed beauty and assurance into my soul. He responded to me powerfully and intimately, and I have never forgotten.

My teenage years flourished and ended like a bountiful

Palouse wheat harvest, with plentiful friendships and college dreams. I set my sights on Seattle Pacific University to obtain a teaching certificate, planning to use my gifts in helping children overcome learning disabilities.

After graduation, I took a temporary job at a cancer research center in Seattle, and I visited my family on holidays in Walla Walla, where I attended my home church, First Presbyterian.

My childhood girlfriend, Erica, also attended there, and I thought that she and the Army guy she was with were dating. Erica only hung out with true Christian gentlemen, and he seemed nice — if you liked his type. I asked about their relationship, and she set me straight.

"We're just friends, thank you. He's into climbing mountains."

"Hmm. I'm thinking about hiking mountains, too," I said.

"No, Karen. I mean he *climbs* them. To the top — like Rainier and Mount St. Helens. He grew up as a wild missionary kid in Thailand."

I was mildly curious to hear his story, and it seemed a happy coincidence to me that Dave Eubank liked the outdoors, since I was embracing my new backpack persona. I planned to frequent every majestic vista on the Seattle horizon.

Dave and I kept running into one another the next couple weeks at church events and sporting goods stores, and he finally convinced me to try a mountain ascent with his climbing partners. The next phase of my training for a

Eubank marriage (on foreign soil) kicked in on the morning I climbed Mount Shuksan. Sinking my ice axe into a mountain face to pull myself toward Dave felt strangely fulfilling, but I didn't dare let on — or admit it to myself at the time.

I wasn't about to let a muscle-bound distraction deter me from landing a career teaching school. I planned to lead a quiet, routine, satisfied life in the suburbs. Dave's uninhibited trust in God captivated me, and I shared his tireless quest for outdoor adventure — but I made it clear that I wasn't interested in romance. We were climbing partners and hiking buddies. Christian friends, that's all.

But I had invited a water buffalo into my well-organized china closet.

In our first months as adventure seekers, I firmly declined Dave's marriage proposal two times — but his prayers and hopes still bubbled like an artesian spring. He knew my answer. It never changed. But it didn't matter.

I reassured myself that Dave's intensity was not compatible with my personality: "What would we share at breakfast? Topics like guns and rock climbing? War stories?"

Away from Dave, I discussed my feelings with God. I had never met a man who mirrored my all-or-nothing commitment to Christ like Dave, and it troubled me that we were becoming soul mates.

Could a woman be in love without giddy school-girl feelings? And if we married (God forbid), how could I keep pace with a Special Forces soldier who road-marched across life? Should I give up the reins of my perceived destiny? After all, I *knew* where God was leading. I had landed a secure teaching job as a special ed teacher in Seattle. My dream had come true.

Dave had chucked his active-duty Army career and enrolled in Fuller Theological Seminary, praying about becoming a *missionary!*

It seemed like the perfect time to cut the ties, once and for all. *But is this what God wants?*

Dave kept in touch with me by telephone, while I drifted in single-adult rhythms with a community of professionals. I planned to meet with Dave at Christmas and reaffirm my decision to remain just "friends."

At Christmas break, Dave cautiously asked if we might begin officially dating, and I surprised myself when my heart wavered. I agreed to Dave's proposal that we call ourselves a couple, presuming that I had plenty of time to know God's will.

Then, during Fuller's spring break, Dave blew into Seattle like a predictable Thai monsoon — this time courting *closure.*

He seemed a little more resigned to his lonely fate as I dodged around the marriage issue at lunch. At my apartment, Dave offered to drive me to Los Angeles on his way back to Pasadena. I accepted out of courtesy, thankful that I had plenty of time to pray and regain my perspective from an unemotional vantage later …

Then the telephone rang, and God turned my world upside down.

"How soon do they want me?"

His demeanor changed. He seemed to be receiving orders for some classified mission.

Dave hung up the phone, and a smile played on his lips.

"Karen, I need to talk to you."

I had been eavesdropping on *our* call to serve the people of Burma.

On a quiet, meaningful stroll on the white sands of Carmel we poured out exactly how we felt about one another — no holds barred.

Dave seemed uncharacteristically reflective, as if we stood together on the eve of a critical op. We flopped to the sand, and I scooted close, leaning against him. We were as silent as moonlight glinting off the waves.

I had said all that there was to say — to God and to myself. I had made a decision.

"I don't want to live without you, Dave. As for marrying you — can you let me sleep on it?"

Dave's friend in Carmel had offered us accommodations, and he showed us to our rooms after a late-night snack. I lay wide awake in my bed, mesmerized by the rhythmic surf outside. Dave needed my answer by daylight, and I wrestled one last time as I tried to picture what the future might look like with my handsome moonlight soldier.

I tried on the name "Karen Eubank" and felt pride bloom in my soul. But, could I get along with this intense man? I had never even been on a short-term overseas trip with my church. What did a missionary do, anyway?

Suddenly, a steep wave of divinely inspired determination swamped my thoughts.

Marrying Dave is my path for living as close to God as I possibly can.

I had all the information I needed to make this decision, and I could not live with myself if I refused Dave's proposal. If I had the faith to make this life-altering choice, I would have the faith to see it through. God was offering me a great gift — not only a deep friendship, but a *purpose*. I drifted off to sleep, content. I was following Jesus into a satisfying partnership and mission.

I awoke feeling elated. Free! Months of turmoil and uncertainty gone. It was April 4 when I officially consented to date Dave until our marriage on the beach at Malibu two and a half months later.

☙☙☙

I couldn't keep my eyes off the machete in the renegade soldier's belt. He stood eye to eye with Dave, holding Dave's wrist, and I sidled away from the two men behind me. The humid air turned electric as Dave broke Machete Man's grasp.

Lightning quick, he grabbed Machete Man's wrist, twisted it and shoved it into the man's chest. Grimacing, Machete Man stumbled back a pace. Veins in Dave's neck bulged as he stepped toward the three soldiers.

He raised a fist in the air, and his threats in English needed no interpretation.

"Karen." Dave lowered his voice, and our eyes met for an instant. "Walk. Walk!" He pointed to the trail *not* suggested by the drunken trio.

I hated to leave Dave, but his "mad killer" scheme seemed to be working. I strode briskly away, glancing over my shoulder while Dave continued scolding the soldiers. I was about to round a corner and lose sight of them, when I paused. Dave was backing away, and I continued my prayer for his safety. They didn't follow him, and he quickly caught up, propelling my rucksack and me, glancing behind us over and over.

The renegade soldiers weren't ready to bleed or die for the chance of stealing anything from this bold tourist. My heart still thrashed as Dave said, "Hopefully there aren't more soldiers with guns around here. Let's double-time it."

But the next soldier we met did have a gun. It was rare to see a man in this part of the country wearing a wristwatch, and immediately Dave knew that he was a Wa Army officer. My eyes were glued to the soldier's sidearm as we showed proper deference.

Dave asked him in Wa, "Can you tell us which way to Thao Mae?"

He nodded and pointed. We were on the right road, and I almost hugged the stern little man before we hurried off.

RANGERS IN THE GAP

I underestimated the shock and awe that a 20-something schoolteacher from Seattle would face on a primitive Asian frontier. I followed Dave in a dream world of aching muscles and interrupted sleep, populated by curious women, frightened children and grim-faced opium and rice farmers. Every Wa headman in a village welcomed us with his wife's rice dish so spiced with chilies that my digestive tract screamed for relief — over and over all night.

In quiet moments, I marveled at this partner I was learning to adore. Animated by reckless compassion, Dave and I were discovering together that loving impoverished people of every religion, ethnic group, political persuasion, gender and personality satisfied our craving to serve Jesus. Neither of us had ever experienced such fulfillment. Whether sponging goop from a child's eyes or lancing a boil, we included a short prayer for every patient in the name of the One who sent us.

The poor but generous Wa families opened their homes to us without reservation, and Dave's political savvy played like notes in a symphony among our hosts. Headmen in the villages valued his grasp of the politics affecting the whole nation of Burma.

Sometimes I felt annoyed that Dave found *his* missionary work so stimulating. Often campfires died to embers, and I dozed off while political and religious discussions glowed until dawn. Only months before, I had been a career-oriented special ed teacher — respected among my colleagues. Who was I now?

DEFINING OUR MISSION

In my bone-weary condition, I asked myself, *I'm comfortable playing second fiddle, but will I ever use my teaching talents again?*

Our conversations with U Saw Lu, the Wa leader whose visit to Allan Eubank launched our mission to the Wa State, touched Dave deeply — and shocked me.

U Saw Lu was a follower of Jesus Christ. Years before, he had collaborated with the U.S. Drug Enforcement Administration (DEA) to implicate a regional Wa drug lord in drug trafficking. Lu was captured by the SLORC (State Law and Order Restoration Council), the ruling dictatorship of Burma, and imprisoned. He was tortured upside down during nearly two months of captivity by SLORC secret police.

When the Wa Army threatened to mount an attack to free U Saw Lu, the secret police released him. Though infirm from his ordeal, Lu renewed his mission to eradicate opium dependency in his homeland.

In 1993, U Saw Lu gathered 500 like-minded Wa soldiers as a security force and broke through Tatmadaw lines and marched south. He presented his plan to stop all opium production in the Wa State to UN and U.S. officials. Lu called his ambitious program "The Bondage of Opium: The Agony of the Wa People, a Proposal and Plea."

At the time of his proposal, the United Wa State Army savored a tentative cease-fire with the Tatmadaw. The UWSA was well-trained and equipped — but financed by opium. No other state or division in all of Burma had the money to keep the generals of the SLORC from invading and controlling their sovereign territories.

But the UN refused to protect the Wa during Saw Lu's proposed three-year opium-to-rice transition period, and the United States rejected his plea for financial aid. Once again, the Wa leaders were thrust upon the horns of a moral dilemma.

Horn 1.) Change their economy from opium to rice on their own, risking poverty, brutality to families and torture of dissidents by the Tatmadaw.

Horn 2.) Allow the poppy growers and corruption to finance the United Wa State Army, to stave off the SLORC's control of their Wa State.

U Saw Lu turned to God for wisdom and met with Wa refugees in Chiang Mai. A Wa church flourished there, and from Chiang Mai, U Saw Lu broadcast an invitation for missionaries to come and "share the light of Jesus Christ with the Wa people." The Wa church prayed that compassion and love would supplant greed and fear in their land.

Lu visited a trusted missionary named Allan Eubank, whose son had resigned his commission as a Major in the U.S. Army Special Forces.

One look at a picture of David Eubank in his Special Forces beret and Lu told Allan, "That's what we need. He's a warrior. Our people are a warrior people. They will understand him. Send him."

And perhaps this son of Pastor Eubank might use his

connections in the United States to persuade the powerful government to reconsider his "proposal and plea," to free his people from the immoral chains of greed and opium.

Closed Door

On our second trip to the Wa State during Dave's summer break from Fuller, I felt better prepared for our expedition. We carried medical supplies specific to Wa needs. We taught hands-on seminars about hygiene and first aid, along with Bible courses in Christian leadership.

I could deliver a single grain of rice to my lips with chopsticks and sleep soundly in a room with a dozen strangers. I could smile while standing in a truck with 30 sweaty men holding M-16 rifles. I could even eat the baby chick floating in a bowl of porridge and nod approvingly to our delighted host.

My mind and body were tempered for hard climbs in humid 100-degree heat or fording muddy streams while buckets of rain poured through my hair. The only time it didn't rain was between the hours of 5 and 7 a.m.

Yet, whenever Dave and I hiked to villages without armed security escorts, a fear of making life-and-death decisions haunted me. What if Dave was captured by the Tatmadaw or was bitten by a viper? How could I save him? Which trail would I choose to find help?

As a busy teacher, reading C.S. Lewis on a grassy knoll at Washington's Discovery Park without a soul in sight thrilled me. I cherished solitude. But in the jungles of

Burma, anxieties at being alone gnawed at my faith.

One day, hours away from our village destination, Dave fell ill, and I felt panic. Dry heaves were weakening him, and he lay against his heavy pack breathing like he had finished a steep ascent. I prayed for his healing. I prayed for myself.

God? I don't know what to do.

I knelt on the leafy, wet trail, dabbing sweat from my husband's forehead, and realized that if I wallowed in evil scenarios, I would be no good to Dave — especially if he took a turn for the worse. I battled hard, pushing back dread while I waited out the hours.

Finally, Dave showed signs of recovery, and we resumed our march slowly.. We arrived at the village where Dave was able to regain his strength.

I value these lessons during my first missionary journeys, like heirlooms given me by a loving father. God was teaching me that battles in my mind decided victories in the world around me. I dared not allow fear to replace faith at crucial moments.

In the Wa jungle and mountains, Dave and I framed lasting templates for our relationship. We shared our loads, adjusted our pace and climbed together. Dave proved faithful and caring to his girl from Walla Walla, and I proved supportive and willing to learn — unshakeable in my commitment to God and my beloved soldier.

ॐॐॐ

DEFINING OUR MISSION

Dave and I rode an exciting wave of purpose after his graduation at Fuller. At Chiang Mai, we prepped for our third mission, packing extra supplies for Dave's father, a medical missionary, and a friend whose family members evangelized the Wa in the 1900s. Even journalists joined our ministry troop, and it seemed that God was shining the light upon the Wa State.

But as quickly as our Wa ministry began, the open door suddenly slammed shut.

The dictatorship that ruled Burma with an iron fist (the SLORC) pressured Wa leaders to close entry to all foreigners — especially to an ex-Special Forces soldier, his well-connected father and journalists.

What problems might this Eubank contingent stir up among Wa Christians? What if Christian virtues took root in the Tatmadaw's opium society? And how might sensitive heroin markets in the United States and Europe react to an exposé by journalists about their expanding narcotics distribution?

Deflated and restless, Dave and I maintained contact with U Saw Lu and our Christian friends in the Wa State through a strong Wa church in Chiang Mai. Meanwhile, we grappled with our roles as missionaries all over again.

Karen State in Brief

Burma (Myanmar) has been called The Golden Land because of its thousands of gilded idols and shrines. It is presently divided into 14 provinces with seven states representing seven races and seven other divisions. These distinctive ethnic states have struggled to maintain their independence from Burman dynastic rulers for centuries.

Burma is also home to one of the world's longest-running civil wars.

The five million Karen State citizens along the Thai-Burma border are some of the most exploited and abused people on earth. Living in tribal societies and governed by chiefs and princes, the Karen roots in South and Eastern Burma date back to the seventh century.

The Karen welcomed European Christian missionaries who brought literacy and education during the British colonial rule, but most Karens today still worship as Buddhists and Animists.

In World War II, during the Japanese occupation of Burma, the Karen joined British and American forces as guerrilla fighters. After the war, Britain granted independence to all 14 provinces in Burma, and the Karen celebrated as a sovereign nation — until a powerful Burman military government based in Rangoon declared all states and frontier areas absorbed into the "Union of Burma."

A well-equipped Burma Army, later known as the Tatmadaw, marched against Karen villages to subdue any opposition to their tyrannical control. Outgunned and outnumbered, Karen freedom fighters were driven deep into the jungles.

By 1962, the Burmese Army pocked the Karen State with permanent camps and relocation villages. Freedom fighters and their families fled to the jungles to live as fugitives in their own homeland.

Missionaries from neighboring nations crossed the border into the Karen State to help these displaced people. Christians believed and taught that their message of hope could change the hearts of soldiers, freedom fighters and even leaders of a vicious military junta.

Free the Oppressed

From hostels that cared for missionaries, children and travelers, Dave and I stared across the international border into the Karen State where the Tatmadaw intimidated and abused villagers.

For several restless months, Dave and I had been teaching at churches and serving at hostels just across the Burma border.

Refugees spoke in worried tones about a new offensive in the Karen State where their loved ones lived. The Tatmadaw had fortified its positions — a signal that they were preparing to invade the frontier again.

Every few years Burma battalions burned a swath of terror from village to village, cutting off supplies to resistance groups and killing landowners. During each horrific military operation, hundreds of families lost their homes and livelihoods.

In the evenings, after church services, refugees told us about the atrocities they had suffered, and I could see Dave's indignation boiling. Karen women and children trickled over the border bearing stories of indiscriminate murder, forced labor and torture.

Through official channels, the Burma dictatorship had threatened Dave, too. He had entered Burma illegally; therefore, if they caught him inside their borders, *he would never leave.*

The U.S. Army Special Forces motto, De Oppresso Liber (Free the Oppressed), smoldered in Dave's soul, and only his missionary paradigm kept it from igniting.

After his banishment from his wild Wa country, Dave questioned why God had sidelined him. I fretted, too, knowing how close Dave was to chucking his missionary work and going back to what he believed would fulfill him: Army life. Tomorrow, I might be an Army major's wife — a complete reversal of my own direction.

We wrangled within our emotions and prayed together, knowing that God had sent us to Burma and feeling uneasy about leaving missionary work behind. Dave and I lived in a small house in Chiang Mai when we felt God suddenly reaffirming our shared calling.

I had been gifted with three beautiful sisters when I married Dave: Ruth, Laurie and Suewannee. Pete Dawson, Dave's boyhood friend (and fighting partner in Bangkok), had married Laurie, and he traveled as a U.S. Naval commander. Laurie and her two children, Sarah and Dave, lived in Thailand between Pete's duty stations. I was clueless about Asian customs and behaviors, and Laurie, who understood the culture, became my mentor and soul sister.

Dave and I were very open with Laurie, about how we struggled to find God's will. It was through my soul sister that God's strong, yet gentle, command pointed us back to Burma.

Go to Rangoon, and see Aung San Suu Kyi.

During Laurie's prayer and quiet times, day and night, these words echoed in her soul — prompting her to speak to Dave. To confirm this very real call to "see Aung San Suu Kyi," Laurie asked for prayer and counsel from Christian friends and family as well.

As a student, Laurie had studied East Asian History and Sociology/Anthropology. Reading the works of Gandhi and Martin Luther King had awakened her interest in non-violent protests, and Burma's 8888 Uprising had inspired Laurie to learn more about Burma's democracy icon and her ideals.

"Dave, we should go see Aung San Suu Kyi. The Burma government is allowing her to receive visitors at her home in Rangoon now."

Dave respected Suu Kyi, too, and he knew many resistance fighters in Burma who hoped that she would help them gain independence from the Burma government *if* she landed a legitimate position in parliament.

Dave seemed to come alive at the idea of talking to Suu Kyi, like his sister had challenged him to a Class 5 technical climb.

Suu Kyi's father, General Aung San, had been a

national hero who negotiated Burma's independence from the British Empire after World War II. Aung San was assassinated in 1947 by Burmese political rivals, and Suu Kyi's mother, Khin Kyi, became ambassador to India and Nepal under the new Burma dictatorship.

With degrees in philosophy, politics and economics, Suu Kyi followed her parents' ideals into public life. Suu Kyi spearheaded the National League for Democracy (NLD) and, after elections, emerged as a beloved political leader. Her NLD party won 80 percent of the seats in Burma's parliament, but the ruling dictatorship nullified the results of the landmark election. The Tatmadaw crushed peaceful demonstrations, and the blood of protesters ran in the streets.

A reshuffled military junta offered Suu Kyi freedom to leave Burma, but she refused. They put her under house arrest at her childhood home on Inya Lake in Rangoon (Yangon). For the next 15 years, Suu Kyi suffered the loss of family and freedoms.

"How could I ever get into Rangoon?" Dave mused. "They'll never give me permission. As soon as I get off the plane, they'll arrest me."

"We should apply for approval and see what God does. You *need* to talk to Suu Kyi, Dave."

Laurie was resolute. Dave was buoyant. But all I could think of was the last threat from the SLORC — if they ever caught Dave, they said they would "finish him."

After much prayer, and without a single hitch in Dave

and Laurie's strategy, Burma travel permits came through. Laurie even made reservations at the Academy Hotel, close to Suu Kyi's house on Inya Lake. Brother and sister planned to stay one week and find a way to contact Suu Kyi as God led them.

Dave and Laurie flew off to Rangoon like two soldiers on a mission, while I fought back tears of helpless concern. A week passed without knowing my husband's and Laurie's fate, but once again, God had everything under control. Through communications with ethnic Christians on both sides of the border, supporters in Rangoon assisted Dave and Laurie and helped them with their mission.

Was it hubris that compelled Dave to visit Suu Kyi? Did he really believe he could help heal the wounds of abused people caught in a war of cultures?

Dave asked these questions of himself as he sat in a hotel room 200 yards from Suu Kyi's former prison home.

During long hours waiting for the opportunity to speak with Suu Kyi, Laurie and Dave plotted an escape in case the secret police were to burst through their barricaded door. The two planned to dive into the lake from the veranda and swim to a foreign embassy 100 yards away.

As for landing an interview with Burma's iconic democracy leader, it appeared impossible. Literally thousands lined up at her gate on the weekends to hear Suu Kyi's speeches — under the watchful eyes of the secret police and video cameras. The Tatmadaw's trucks parked strategically on University Avenue, likely concealing machine guns for "crowd control." The dictators seemed well prepared to crush free expression in the city, as well as on the Burma frontiers.

That Friday, Dave and Laurie knocked on Suu Kyi's locked front yard gate to try for an appointment to speak with her. Time was running out. Their flight home was scheduled for Sunday.

"Suu Kyi is not available for interviews on weekends. I'm sorry ..."

Lord?

Dave and Laurie walked back to their hotel, wondering, but clinging to a thread of hope: The attendant had given Dave Suu Kyi's personal phone number.

Dave prayed with Laurie. "Jesus, if this is *my* misguided attempt at helping this nation, I give it all up. If I can't get an appointment with Suu Kyi, we know you want us to go home."

Not long after praying, Dave tried to call and spoke directly to Suu Kyi! He set an appointment to visit with her in person on Monday.

Laurie had made a previous commitment to arrive home on Sunday, but Dave changed his flight to a later date. Laurie's burden to "see Aung San Suu Kyi" lifted, and peace flooded her heart, knowing that she had obeyed God and that Dave was fulfilling God's purposes.

When Dave handed his passport to military intelligence at the gate to Suu Kyi's home without being arrested, he felt like the Red Sea had parted. In her sitting room, Suu Kyi shared her vision for a free and democratic nation, and Dave offered his experience and services to be an ambassador of peace to help unite the people of Burma.

Dave asked if he could pray with her, and Suu Kyi welcomed it. Then he gave her his personal Bible that he had received at ordination. She asked Dave to tell pastors everywhere to pray for Burma and quoted a favorite verse: "You shall know the truth, and the truth shall set you free ..." (John 8:32).

Suu Kyi expressed her deepest hope for unity between Burmans and all ethnic people — and unity among the diverse ethnic groups themselves.

Before parting, Dave placed his Special Forces insignia in Suu Kyi's delicate fingers: a beret pin with crossed arrows and a sword upon a shield. She took the crest smiling and read the inscription aloud: *De Opresso Liber* (Free the Oppressed).

On this mission my beloved husband received his marching orders: a piercing confirmation that he still complied with his Commander's Intent. His coordinates were set correctly after all — to Burma!

Dave flew home to me safe and sound, where God began to equip us for an exciting 20-year odyssey of faith. No climb has ever been so exhilarating, no terrain so uncertain. We faced a probing soul-searching that shaped our characters for loving and leading close friends and our own children through landmines and mortar fire. In less than a year after Dave's meeting with Suu Kyi, ethnics and Burmans would know us as Free Burma Rangers.

A secular warrior might have engaged the Tatmadaw with deadly force to rescue defenseless villagers hiding in the Karen jungle. Instead, he tramped to the frontlines with a rucksack crammed with food, children's toys and medical supplies. Tireless, genuine and inspiring, Dave drafted everyone he met into his orbit of loving people unconditionally. He called everyone he met to experience freedom by forgiving — and his message inspired many who heard, whether Buddhist, Christian, resistance fighter or enemy. No one Dave spoke with escaped his urgent plea to help him overcome evil with good. (No neutral ground exists in his world.)

Dave began forging a set of personal rules of engagement for his missions: *Never surrender. Never leave the defenseless to suffer alone. ALWAYS stake a position between unprotected people and the advancing Tatmadaw.*

సావసావసా

But while Dave studied his new orders of operations, I struggled with my own role as wife and missionary. I traveled with Dave at every opportunity, but more often I stayed in Chiang Mai, helping our organization with administrative duties. And that *wasn't* what I signed up for. More and more projects multiplied from Dave's exciting meetings with ethnic leaders, and the paperwork sometimes buried me. I realized that my usefulness as a missionary and my fulfillment depended upon conquering one grueling mountain in my path: the Thai language. I began learning Thai to become effective as a friend and evangelist and to use my gift as a teacher.

During our 1996 watershed year, a meeting with Suu Kyi's close friend (an influential senator) led to a Global Day of Prayer for Burma, spearheaded by Dave's parents and Laurie. For the first time, newsletters, broadcasts and the prayers of millions cast a light on the plight of ethnics brutalized by the Burma Army.

People of all faiths petitioned God for peace among ethnics and Burmans, armed and unarmed. We prayed for all races to be treated as equals in a genuine union that recognized the rule of law and human rights. This yearly prayer meeting has continued for 17 years!

I felt humbled to help my mentors break ground as they confronted evil as powerfully as anyone evangelizing in the most violent jungle regions. Keeping company with these beautiful, determined missionaries taught me to seize the reins of my own calling and later fulfill my purpose, too.

Freedom Conference

What border?

Dave spent weeks hiking unarmed through the Burma jungle and across mountain passes to speak directly to resistance leaders, politicians and village headmen. Before Free Burma Rangers existed, ethnics had no idea who this stealthy "soldier of fortune" was. His personal friendships with other freedom fighters and his own name, Eubank, gained him access to wary guerrilla leaders and fearful villagers.

"Don't shoot!"

Dave's modus operandi in approaching guerrilla camps was to accost sentries with a friendly "*haloo*" before they opened up with M-16s. With hands in plain view, he asked sentries to bear a message to the commander of each resistance unit about his mission.

Dave carried exciting news of a secret ethnic unity conference to be held in the Eastern Karen State and explained that funds would be available to help their delegates make the trip. The conference was the first of its kind, and word spread like wildfire. Leaders in every state and division wanted someone from their own ethnic group to represent them.

More than 100 delegates arrived for the Ethnic Nationalities Seminar at Mae Tha Ra Hta, a two-week conference, which Dave coordinated. Delegates were strategically situated together so that they had opportunity to hash out differences over campfires and tea.

The main meeting took place in a Buddhist monastery, and Dave's role was to make each delegate feel welcome. He opened with silent prayer among all major religions and races when the meetings convened each day.

A 13-point document incorporated their hopes for a federal union of Burma. The ethnic leaders tentatively agreed to support Aung San Suu Kyi as their candidate for prime minister of Burma, and everyone left with a sense of purpose and unprecedented cooperation. One Buddhist delegate from the Pa'O tribe told Dave, "Your God won. Your God was here." (These ethnic unity meetings have continued every year since 1996.)

The following year, in 1997, the Burma military junta abolished the State Law and Order Restoration Council (SLORC) and reorganized as a more potent State Peace and Development Council (SPDC).

David Eubank's name headlined a fresh SPDC "enemy of the state" list, while the Tatmadaw mounted one of the bloodiest offensives in history against our frontier neighbors. Karen, Karenni and Shan families fled to the mountains and jungles to escape systematic, unrelenting torture and murder by soldiers trained by the Burma central government.

The small, ill-equipped Karen, Karenni and Shan resistance forces collapsed, and a steady stream of 11,000 villagers funneled into one route, filling refugee camps to overflowing.

I was safely, but unhappily, secure in Chiang Mai during this Tatmadaw offensive when Dave began fulfilling his Commander's Intent, fighting evil with hand-to-hand compassion.

Birth of a Vision

Dave crept from an abandoned hostel on the Burma border where, days before, children played on swing sets in a schoolyard. Climbing a stony cliff nearby, distant explosions echoed from the west. Below him, a quarter-mile-long queue of men and women stumbled silently like pack animals, loaded with sacks of rice looted from a refugee camp. Tatmadaw soldiers prodded and coaxed their slaves, and none dared to cry out.

At Dave's feet, a trampled flag lay in the dirt, and he decided to drive home a point: The Burma Army ignored international rules at will. He snapped a few photos, raised the neighboring nation's flag on a bamboo pole and hollered to get the soldiers' attention.

"Do the right thing! Let them all go! Bless you —"

Pinging bullets cut short my husband's words. He skittered behind boulders and off the hill like a mountain goat.

At his truck a safe distance away, Dave packed four rucksacks with medical supplies and hoisted two of them on his shoulders for an arduous five-hour march to a crowded IDP camp where ill and injured families were said to be hiding.

When a guerrilla carrying an M-16 suddenly materialized from a side trail a few feet away, Dave sized up the KNLA (Karen National Liberation Army) soldier. He was totally kitted out for combat, and two grenades hung from an ammo harness across his chest. In one ear a blood-red ruby set in gold glinted brightly. But it wasn't the pirate's earring that held Dave's attention — it was his broad smile.

"My name is Eliya. I'm a medic. How can I help you?" He spit crimson-colored betel nut juice on the ground. He spoke in English, and Dave glanced at four refugee men standing nearby. They were staring, too.

Dave explained his destination, a little wary, and the man suddenly grabbed one of his packs. He nodded to the strapping refugees standing, watching. "You can run away later. But for now, help us."

By the time Dave left his pickup, God had provided four men and a human rights journalist to help carry supplies with Dave and Eliya, God's medic. The group pressed through a human tide of refugees using their same trails, while Eliya treated malaria or gunshot wounds along the way.

At the IDP camp, they found more than 1,000 people huddled in groups around campfires and in dilapidated bamboo huts.

For four days, Dave and Eliya cared for the sick and wounded. Fatherless children shivered from malaria and typhus on wet blankets. Women traumatized by rape hugged their knees staring into nothingness. Men guarded little piles of keepsakes like gold. And everywhere, injured internally displaced people (IDPs) bandaged with dirty strips from sarongs moaned in anguish.

When Dave and Eliya ran out of medical supplies, they melted into the jungle like the morning mist. They crossed deeply into Burma to recon Tatmadaw positions, praying often that the Burma Army might never remember the trails leading to the IDP camp. And God answered.

Dave and Eliya's incursion of mercy became a prototype for strategies in saving the lives of thousands of

IDPs in Burma. Soon an army of love-motivated men and women would rally to God's call, some by giving time and funds, others by risking their lives to help these forgotten people.

It was dusk when God's two weary soldiers finally arrived at Dave's pickup again. They were resting on the tailgate when two Karen ethnics stumbled into the road carrying a wounded man in a sling attached to a bamboo pole.

"Please! Can you help us?"

They asked Dave to transport their wounded friend to a hospital six hours away. The young man had stepped on a landmine, and shreds of his mangled muscle and bone smelled of gangrene. Eliya rigged two IVs from the pickup's roll-bar above the patient, then shook Dave's hand.

"I need to find my family now," he said. "Maybe next week I will be dead! We were separated when the Burma Army came. My wife and son were with friends, and I'm trusting God to take care of them."

Touched by Eliya's selflessness and compassion, Dave prayed for the Karen soldier as he shouldered his M-16. Dave gave him a Special Forces coin as a token of friendship, and Eliya disappeared into the gloom, never thinking he would see the white missionary warrior again.

Neither man fathomed that the Karen pirate was God's first Free Burma Ranger.

An exciting idea rappelled into Dave's heart after he returned home.

DEFINING OUR MISSION

Only one power on earth could motivate people to face this raw brutality, and that was God's LOVE. What if we build an army of men and women like Eliya — willing to confront evil in the jungles of Burma, not with machetes and guns, but with love and compassion?

Churches in Asia and in the United States prayed for the healthy birth of our vision. On a family furlough in Alaska, the theme of our humanitarian movement appeared like the first glimpse of our nation's tallest peak. For R&R (Rest and Recuperation), Dave prepared for a well-planned technical ascent of 20,000-foot Denali (Mount McKinley).

When park rangers asked, "What's the name of your climbing group, sir?" Dave was speechless for an instant — then it came to him.

"We're the Free Burma Rangers!"

The simple name summed up our desire to provide relief and love to the desperate people in Burma.

In this radical life with my beloved soldier of grace, I still revel in *living as close to God as I possibly can.*

For the first five years of my missionary life, I spent little time in Burma. While Dave penetrated the jungle on solitary forays, I stayed at our home in Chiang Mai, studying the Thai language and culture and coordinating media projects.

Since then, I have often filled rucksacks with children and provisions, to follow Dave into the remote Karen State and beyond.

Dave marks his first IDP experience with Eliya as the milestone that crystallized our mission as Free Burma Rangers:

"To bring help, hope and love to people of all faiths and ethnicities in conflict zones of Burma, to shine a light on the actions of oppressors, to stand with the oppressed and support leaders and organizations committed to liberty, justice and service."

Deploying this vision all over the world has become our passion.

Maternal Chapters

I mark three maternal chapters that defined my own purpose here in Asia. The birth of Sahale, our first beautiful daughter, in Anchorage while on furlough, challenged old interpretations of my role as missionary.

My instinct to nurture Sahale immediately clashed with vital ministries like writing newsletters and bookkeeping. Chores threatened to gobble up precious bonding time with Sahale, like an insatiable time python.

My daughter needed a full-time mommy to prepare for jungle trips, and I gave up office duties to my capable and Godly friend, Amy Galetzka. Amy was our very first Ranger volunteer (serving from 1999 until today!), and she remains key in FBR operations. Eliya Samson became uncle to Sahale, and later to Suuzanne and Peter, and worked as a versatile assistant and facilitator. These two wonderful groundbreakers opened the way for many more Free Burma Rangers who have loved our children as they have loved Dave and me.

Dave deferred to my wisdom at the time and trusted my decisions completely — one more cherished component that strengthened our unconventional partnership. He treasured my commitment to raising our first child — his little White Monkey — the pet name given Sahale by our Free Burma Rangers.

"Suuzanne" was the title of my second maternal chapter, written two years after the Tatmadaw withdrew its troops from near the Thai-Burma border to plague ethnics in Northern Burma. The Tatmadaw left behind many new permanent camps in the Karen State from which their battalions could mobilize.

The Karen National Liberation Army (KNLA) and other paramilitary groups developed an intricate surveillance network to track the Tatmadaw day by day. Villages could be alerted when Tatmadaw units marched, and residents often had time to bury their rice sacks, gather a few belongings and flee before soldiers burned their homes.

My strenuous marches into Burma with Dave and the girls became more frequent and asked for by ethnics we visited. Protected by resistance fighters, we traveled to the northern reaches of the Karen State to break ground for a Free Burma Rangers training center. God was stirring up people to fight the Tatmadaw in a new way: by bringing relief and love to the IDPs surviving in the jungles and mountains.

Dave and a few part-time Burma Rangers built our first single-room bamboo hut with a porch for our family to live in. Because of Dave's rapport with the regional leaders, many in their guerrilla ranks came for training at the new boot camp shaped by powerful Biblical principles.

At first, Dave's code puzzled hardcore soldiers, Buddhist monks and villagers. His vision seemed plausible: *To free the oppressed and to stand for human dignity, justice and reconciliation in Burma.*

But, for men and women whose families had been brutalized, the FBR mission statement was harder to swallow: *To bring help, hope and love to people of ALL faiths and ethnicities ...*

When he heard that Eliya Samson had been killed, Dave felt heartbroken — but the rumor was false! So when he ran into the bejeweled pirate again, only a bear hug could show his feelings. Eliya had been independently treating refugees and IDPs, and Dave immediately set out to recruit him to help him form up the Free Burma Rangers.

Dave invited men and women from all Burma states — including Karen, Karenni, Shan, Pa'O, Arakan, Kachin, Chin and Lahu — to join the Free Burma Rangers, if they were willing to put aside cultural hatred against one another and especially against the Burmans.

The Free Burma Rangers offered ethnics a new and better way to fight: with God's love. Dave respected each man's right to protect himself and the IDPs with firearms, but the FBR policy was rigid: *Never* initiate a fight.

With every pushup, every song and every suture, Dave embedded the FBR rationale for loving the IDPs and *anyone* enslaved by evil: *Jesus is real. Jesus is the Savior. Jesus offers a better way to fight and ultimately win.*

At any moment, Dave might stop and pray for help in a decision, or physical healing, or attitude adjustment among Rangers. He dedicated every planning session to Jesus, which set the tone for all training and every mission.

My third maternal chapter opened with the birth of our son, Peter. My treks with Dave had seasoned me but also wearied me. Both daughters had bouts with serious fevers, and I feared for my baby boy, too. Peter was 3 weeks old when I carried him with the girls (aboard their "backpack uncles") deep into Burma on a three-month mission to help IDPs. I shared laughter and fears with other nursing mothers with children in their bamboo homes or on trails where they were trying to survive.

Love *proved* became love received.

More than 100,000 IDPs lived a subsistence lifestyle in the jungles and mountains years after the '97 offensive. Destitute families built primitive settlements with hidden gardens and schools. At a moment's notice they might be warned to flee an advancing Tatmadaw battalion.

I had discovered an ability to create a home for my family wherever we lived or worked — whether as guests in luxurious houses during furloughs or at campfires in damp jungle huts.

Dave and our Rangers refurbished our dwelling at the FBR training camp (we stayed there for about three months each year) and added a full story to accommodate our growing family.

After each six-week FBR training session, Dave led a new mission wherever bullets and mortars were falling on or near IDPs.

Our Ranger teams included a team leader, medic, photographer, videographer and children's ministers. Often local people helped us keep track of Tatmadaw movements and contacted resistance groups in the area for logistical support.

My role evolved into traveling with escorts to villages which had schools and supplying what little materials my friends and I could carry for classrooms. Most important, I supplied encouragement and love to the dedicated teachers. My gentle porters helped carry my kids on the miles of trails between villages.

A blanket of depression often draped the hearts of mothers and children, as they faced each day without hope. Most villages had no school building, and the children had little grasp of basic hygiene. Some children had never heard the name of the only One who could secure their eternal destiny — Jesus.

I felt frustrated that I had no lesson plan prepared to supply their knowledge-starved minds. We Rangers needed a way to show IDPs that a good life and peace in the heart were available, no matter if war raged around them.

DEFINING OUR MISSION

As our FBR training season in the Karen State ended, we hiked to the border, then drove to Chiang Mai where the kernel of an idea began to sprout. I prayed for God to help me build a curriculum designed for children to be part of the training of Free Burma Rangers.

I also prayed for Dave's safety on his mission to Dooplaya.

God is merciful to wives. Our premonitions are usually limited to feelings — and not visions. Several hundred miles north, a Tatmadaw officer was screaming to his soldiers, "Kill! Kill!" as Dave dodged a hail of bullets.

And Eliya Samson saved my beloved soldier's life.

CHAPTER 3
LOVE NEVER WASTED
ELIYA SAMSON'S STORY

A story can be written about a man in different shades of opinion, but in trials his true character is revealed.
Eliya Samson — Chief Medic, Free Burma Rangers

Medic's Commission

My eyes felt like gobs of steaming fish paste, and I knew that parasites had invaded my gut. From beneath my soaked headscarf, sweat trickled down my face. As chief medic for the Free Burma Rangers, I would prescribe a feverish patient like me antibiotics and bed rest, but our secret mission had barely begun.

Dave Eubank had folded up the stock on my AK-47 and strapped my weapon to his own rucksack. He also relieved me of 20 pounds of uncooked rice rations, but it didn't help. My legs felt as heavy as teak logs.

Dave prayed for me, and I tried to focus over my shoulder at Doh Say, a Karenni FBR team leader, and Ka Paw Say, our videographer and pastor. Trailing behind them were several porters bearing medical supplies, food, clothing and hygiene essentials.

RANGERS IN THE GAP

Our destination lay across the wide and treacherous Salween River, and our mission was to deliver relief to impoverished members of the mostly Buddhist Pa'O tribe in the Shan State in Northeast Burma.

The Tatmadaw had burned and ransacked Pa'O temples and villages, then ordered the residents to move to a relocation camp. The Pa'O men, women and children were forced to serve the Burma Army as beasts of burden and amusement whenever their battalions marched through their area.

In this part of Burma, the Shan State Army (SSA) had acknowledged the Free Burma Rangers as a non-military humanitarian group. They had assigned a platoon of well-armed SSA soldiers to act as our security force, and for two days we had been avoiding the Tatmadaw like malaria.

Now we hiked through Wa territory, inhabited by rice and opium farmers, where the United Wa State Army (UWSA) fought on the side of the Tatmadaw. The two cultures despised one another, but the UWSA and Tatmadaw shared a common motivation to help one another: *opium money.*

At a base camp before our mission, an SSA general had aimed a finger in our faces. "You do not fire on any Wa (UWSA) soldiers! Understand? We (the SSA) have negotiated with the Wa for your safe passage.

"Don't be seen, and don't shoot back if they fire at you. The Wa know you are escorted by our troops. If they do see you, scatter and hide! We don't want to fight the Wa.

Don't fire back or you might be butchered like a flock of chickens."

The SSA security team, the porters and our Rangers crossed a car road, and I staggered after Dave as he splashed to the far side of a stream, holding his boots in his hands. He flopped to the bank, and everyone followed his lead, spreading out along the creek like thirsty deer.

"You okay, Eliya?" Dave asked me. I nodded, feeling queasy.

"We'll take a break here, Brother."

The main body of our SSA guards filled canteens and marched into a long clearing before disappearing into heavy forest to scout ahead. Then our SSA rear-guard casually crossed the stream to join us.

"Hey! Aren't you our security?" Dave asked, a little testy. Was no one watching behind us?

"No danger. No danger," one of the Shan soldiers said, popping a betel nut into his mouth.

Everyone had let down his guard based upon the word of our SSA escort.

Dave doffed his rucksack and squatted barefoot, filling his canteen in the creek, when out of nowhere a truck skidded up a dust cloud above us 20 yards away. Suddenly bullets from a dozen rifles peppered the bank from positions beside their transport vehicle. A Tatmadaw commander shouted orders, and his subordinates moved toward us.

We were all stunned. We scattered behind trees —

everyone except Dave. Our leader curled up like a rice ball behind his oversized backpack, while bullets spattered the dirt around him.

Dave pulled on socks, then boots, then yanked his laces hard once on each foot before grabbing up his 70-pound pack and running across the clearing. He made a beautiful target.

I crouched behind a banyan tree, my head suddenly cleared by adrenaline. From my first day as a boy on the frontlines, I thrived on split-second life-or-death action — which is one reason I spent years patching up wounded KNLA soldiers. Under fire, in one blink, I could decide to cut or suture to save a life.

Our armed Rangers behind other banyans were obeying orders to the letter. No one fired a shot back at the advancing Wa platoon.

And in seconds I knew that my great friend, David Eubank, would be dead ...

಄಄಄಄

The day I first ran into Dave Eubank in 1997, I had been planning to search refugee camps for my wife, Cat, and my baby son. Dave stood gawking at me when I broke through a bamboo thicket to walk on the car road.

Between battles, our Karen National Liberation Army unit had disbanded for a time to find our displaced families. I had entrusted a friend to care for Cat in a Karen community, but Tatmadaw battalions broke through

KNLA lines and burned his village. My wife fled with thousands of other IDPs and hid in the jungle as she made her way to a refugee camp.

As I watched Dave cramming his last rucksack with medical supplies, I told him, "I'm a medic," and I thought he was going to hug me! He carried potent medications and instruments but had little medical training beyond basic emergency care.

When I agreed to go with him to his destination, a crowded IDP camp, he called me a "pirate-angel."

Thousands of displaced villagers clogged the only car road leading to Thailand from Burma. Parents carrying children and wheeling carts or dragging their belongings plodded to refugee camps several hours away.

Dave and I found time to bandy our opinions about war, politics and God on our way to the IDP camp. We shared our hearts and listened to one another like long-time friends.

The white missionary worked as hard as me, holding IVs and comforting bleeding landmine victims as I dressed their open wounds. And, without exception, the man who would become my teacher and commander prayed for everyone in every circumstance.

Jesus was with me, too, but I seldom spoke to him aloud unless my life hung by a thread. Dave included God in his life on a microscopic level, and he openly gave Jesus credit for keeping every crisis from deteriorating into chaos.

My father was a pastor, too. Reverend Samson had

visited and preached to congregations in a radius of villages around our home near Dooplaya. As a boy, I traveled with my apostle father, attending worship services with my mother and six older siblings.

I inherited my father's compassion and ability to encourage people, and I remember Dad telling me, "Always trust God, Eliya, and be honest. Someday you will be a pastor, too."

I might have been my father's protégé — but the war distracted me. I was staying with my uncle and aunt and attending primary school when the Tatmadaw marched against KNLA positions near their village. The Burma Army killed pig and water buffalo, chicken and dog, as if no creature in the Karen State had a right to live.

Then they shelled my uncle's house.

Mortars fell in the streets, and the *tat-tat* of machine guns terrified me as I hid, watching my relatives' bamboo home burn to cinders. My aunt wept and prayed over my uncle's body, and in my heart a quiet fury marched against the Tatmadaw.

I ran from the scene to find my countrymen on the frontlines, where fathers and sons crouched side by side in bunkers to hold the frontline before Tatmadaw troops overpowered them. Younger children like me carried boxes of ammunition to soldiers, or we helped sustain our fighters with meals of rice. I was 10 years old.

For several months I followed our troops, who could only strike and retreat as the Burma Army forced them off positions. Villages and villagers fell victim to their scorched-earth policy. Then one day the bloodbath against the Karen ended like it began — suddenly and systematically.

In 1981, my school reopened with new subjects: rifle training and hand-to-hand combat. By the age of 14, I was a crack shot with an M-1 carbine, a burgeoning kickboxing champ and proficient in jungle warfare. The Burma Army had built permanent camps near our villages in the Karen State — so I never ran out of Tatmadaw soldiers to harass or kill.

My parents moved to a safer region, and Dad continued pastoring. But like a house built in the rainy season, my own Christian foundation was weak. I carried a Bible in my pocket and prayed in my heart, but I also drank and loved to carouse. I rose in rank in the KNLA and joined in the heaviest fighting, but I felt unsatisfied, no matter what successes I achieved.

In my early 20s, I decided to reset my coordinates. On the frontlines, wounded soldiers cried in agony after landmines severed limbs or shrapnel disfigured them. Sometimes they lay on a blanket for days until a medic came.

If you were a medic, you could help them.

God spoke this clearly to my heart.

I obtained permission from my KNLA commander to train to be a medic. In a refugee camp, I found my beautiful, faithful Cat, and we were married before I left for the frontlines again. She, too, worked in healthcare among our people.

Over the next few years, I gained knowledge in several Burma dialects and learned backcountry dentistry. My father's prayers held me on a course that I never would have chosen. I began opening clinics in villages where their only medicines were herbs and their only physicians, spirit shamans.

Ranger Reunion

Returning to Dave's truck after completing our first mission together at Lay Kon Tu, I thought, *Just being around this soldier-missionary makes me want to be closer to God.*

In one long, hard week we had become fast friends, and I hated to leave him, but I had to find Cat. I stuck his gift to me (his Special Forces coin) deep in my pocket, breathing a prayer that we would meet again.

Cat had evaded capture for weeks, traveling with a group of IDPs and hiding with our tiny son in the jungle. I found my family at a refugee camp, and we moved to a village near Three Pagodas Pass. The nearest Burma Army outpost was a full five miles away.

Our second son was born a year later, and I opened a medical clinic for the local people. I still served in the KNLA, but I stayed home after medical missions on the frontlines.

"Dave Eubank sends word to you, Eliya! He's working at a medical clinic at Three Pagoda Pass."

A man who was passing through our village carried

the message, and I grabbed Cat. "I need to go see my old friend, Dave. I'll be back day after tomorrow, okay?"

Cat frowned a little. My jaunts often ended up longer than I intended. "Promise?" she said.

I kissed Cat and grinned real big.

I stripped down to sandals and shorts and "ran" the 12-hour hike to Three Pagoda in five hours flat! Dave and Karen were unloading medical supplies for their clinic, and I surprised them. I felt like I had found a brother and sister.

During the following two years, Dave and I had grand reunions whenever we met one another on trails or when he brought medicine and other supplies to my village clinic. I traveled to treat more and more refugees and IDPs, even while serving in the KNLA.

Whenever Dave and I spent time together, I peered through a window into Dave's soul, and often he stared into mine.

"I know it seems like a losing battle on the ground," Dave said one day. "The Tatmadaw number about 400,000. The resistance has maybe 15,000 freedom fighters in *all* the provinces together.

"But, Eliya, no dictator can stop us from loving these people. No despot can stop us from serving them. Burma needs people like us who never give up — men and women who will go anywhere, anytime, no matter how dangerous or difficult. Some people sit in a refugee camp or a city complaining about the atrocities. We go to the frontlines and love the people.

"Our battle is not with the Burma Army or their generals. Our fight is with the evil that stirs them to kill their own countrymen."

Dave paused for a moment, then said, "Eliya, I have always wondered why you decided to go on that first trip with me to help IDPs, instead of finding your family."

I thought back to that day and said, "God brought us together, Dave. I was the only medic within many miles. I had peace to go with you. And one thing I have learned in war: When a situation is out of control, don't try to control it. Leave it in God's hands. After the medicine had run out, I felt released to go. I found Cat, and she and my son were safe."

In 2001, my own KNLA commander ordered me to help Dave build his first Free Burma Rangers training camp in the Karen State, and I barely kept the grin off my face.

Our Karen resistance knew every IDP hide site and immediately began aiding the Free Burma Rangers on their relief missions.

Amazing Consensus

Don't fire back ...
A trained soldier tries to think ahead — which is why Dave pulled on his boots in a hail of bullets. Unlike tough-footed ethnics, a bootless white soldier is worthless on a jungle march.

LOVE NEVER WASTED

As Dave ran, a second troop truck pulled up and disgorged more Wa soldiers.

"Thraaaaa!" I screamed after Dave, using the word for "teacher" and fearing I was watching him die.

Dave crammed as many yards between himself and the Wa soldiers as fast as his legs would let him. The Tatmadaw officer's high pitched "Kill! Kill!" frenzied his troops to keep firing at their white quarry, and bullets whizzed past Teacher's ears and between his legs.

Suddenly, one Wa soldier settled down enough to *think.* He switched his AK-47 to automatic, and the first short burst hit three yards to Dave's left side.

Near me a Ranger clutched his own AK-47 to his chest, and while voices all around us warned, "Don't shoot back! Don't shoot back!" I blinked sweat from my eyes and wrenched the weapon from his fingers.

Dave had 10 yards to run before hitting cover, and I heard the second auto burst from an automatic rifle. Bullets whinged three feet from Dave's back. The soldier was "walking" his rounds into his target.

I stepped from behind my banyan tree, took aim with my friend's AK-47 and pulled the trigger — *click.* No round fired, and I jacked a shell into the chamber, aimed again and the semi-auto jerked six times.

Now *I* was the target! An AK burst chipped tree bark near my head. I glanced to where Dave had been and hopped behind the banyan, relieved. The only thing injured was Dave's pride. He hunkered behind a rock, flanked by SSA soldiers who had heard the firefight and returned to "protect" us. Our reinforcements sprayed bullets at the Wa soldiers, and suddenly the trucks spun away with most of their troops.

Warily, we took stock of our creek-side conflict, shaking our heads. Along with four Wa casualties, the Tatmadaw officer lay in a bloody heap.

Dave gathered the SSA soldiers, his FBR men and the porters — and prayed: "God, forgive us ... we pray that we'll see these soldiers in heaven. May we embrace them there as friends. We'll say, 'I'm so sorry you died, but you broke the agreement and tried to kill us! We were sinners, too, and we are *all* here in heaven now, because of the sacrifice and grace of Jesus. You are our dear brothers. We are the same, and we love you ...'"

It was a soldiers' prayer, and we stood silent for a time as reality sunk in. We were in a war zone on a humanitarian mission that was already awash in death. The Tatmadaw or UWSA would track us down for revenge.

"We better move. The whole Burma Army will be here shortly," Dave said solemnly. With full canteens we double-timed toward the Salween River — two day's march away.

But I was feeling better. My fever had broken. And our Teacher would go home to Karen and his children *alive.*

On the banks of the Salween River, nearly 100 of us, SSA soldiers and FBR relief workers, gazed at the ridge we had traversed, all feeling the same: If the Tatmadaw found us, they could rain mortars upon us like aiming at fish in a barrel. The SSA commander had radioed to Wa base camp and explained about the "misunderstanding" at the creek, and the Wa command seemed satisfied. They blamed the dead Tatmadaw officer for the carnage.

"But the Burma Army isn't so forgiving," the SSA leader said. Staring across the quarter-mile of muddy Salween, he continued, "They've mobilized four battalions to find you. If we're going to cross, this is the best place. And we have a boat."

Three Shan soldiers un-sank a teak longboat hidden in reeds. They unloaded rocks that kept it submerged, and I smiled to myself as I watched fear ripple through our party.

One boat. 100 people.

It would take eight hours, at least, to ferry us plus equipment across the river. Dave gathered us Rangers to pray.

"Lord, we face a choice and need your guidance ..."

Then Dave asked what everyone thought. Should we abort the mission, then regroup back home and take relief to the Pa'O a few months from now?

Dave had important business to attend to — what if it took us *two* months getting out of Burma, dodging the Tatmadaw? We had to travel through the Shan State, the Karenni State and the Karen State.

The surprise attack at the creek weighed heavily on the men, and a heated discussion left us divided down the middle. Perhaps it was wise to go back home.

Finally I spoke my mind, too. "Rangers never give up."

Everyone was silent for a few seconds. "We will just die if we have to. We started this mission, and we must finish it. The Pa'O need us."

Everyone stared at his toes.

Dave suddenly left our group to speak with the SSA security officer. "What do you think we should do?" He got the answer I would have given had I been in charge of the security detail.

"We don't *think*. We follow orders. We go where you go."

Dave nodded. "Can I pray with you all?" Every one of the 80 Buddhist soldiers bowed his head. Dave prayed in Thai, a common language, so that everyone understood. "Lord Jesus, give these men safety ..."

After this prayer with the Shan security men, Dave seemed cheerful. "I feel like God is telling me that I am not responsible for the future. The Pa'O are waiting for help. I think we need to keep going. But, I could be *wrong*."

It struck me as funny. I began to chuckle, and so did everyone else — then like a dam suddenly bursting, we guffawed like Dave had told one of his dumb jokes around a campfire back home.

The Buddhist soldiers stared at us like we were crazy, and fear among our Free Burma Rangers vanished. To the last Ranger, we all agreed that we should complete our mission.

The Burma Army never caught up with us as we paddled across the river in our little teak boat. And we found the Pa'O. Many were ill, and we immediately set up a medical clinic to treat wounds, dysentery, malaria and other jungle ailments that stalked their families. At night our Rangers and Shan soldiers hid in the jungle outside the village, praying that we might complete our not-so-secret mission.

Many of the Buddhist Pa'O tribe members had never seen a Bible before, and it was a privilege to share the story of God's Son, Jesus, the One who loved them enough to die for them. We listened to them, too, as they wept, reliving the horrors suffered at the hands of the Burma Army.

Only God could give the Pa'O joy in a place where no hope existed. I had seen this joy in the faces of enduring Christians all over Burma. It was mystical, other-worldly and powerful.

God confirmed to every Ranger that we had made the right decision in crossing the Salween River.

After double-timing again out of the Wa region, we said farewell and thanks to our Shan security escort and set a blazing pace back to headquarters. Dave arrived home to his wife and children in Chiang Mai, and I returned to Cat and my babies.

Boot Camps

Our first Rangers training complex in the Northern Karen State added bamboo structures and students as we built trust with pro-democracy leaders, headmen and villagers on the frontier.

RANGERS IN THE GAP

At first, only Dave, myself and a couple other Free Burma Rangers slogged through swamps or wended our way through jungles. We followed local soldiers to find IDPs who foraged like animals to survive. But then came Sahale, Suuzanne and Peter. As each of Dave and Karen's children was born, I became a favorite uncle and playmate, as well as protector and packhorse. Wherever Dave and Karen trekked to hide sites, the kids often came, too — on my back or shoulders.

Many KNLA soldiers' relatives lived for years as IDPs, too, and word spread among the pro-democracy groups that these humanitarian missionaries called Free Burma Rangers delivered relief to IDPs *wherever* they lived. Dave, his family and his Rangers also risked their lives to lead abused and weary IDPs hundreds of miles to refugee camps in a neighboring country.

Resistance leaders gave their soldiers special leave to aid in constructing buildings at the training center, and KNLA officers sent men to learn medical and relief techniques — the FBR way. Soldiers and villagers from nearly all the states in Burma trickled into our mess halls, and some became Rangers on a permanent basis.

At training camps, cultures collided among ethnics whose tribes had been at war for centuries. Buddhists, Animists, Atheists, Communists and Christians ate, slept, learned, bantered and debated with Dave and one another during their six-week boot camp. And in the end, they found common ground in bringing relief to IDPs. Immediately after our trainees graduated from the physical and technical Ranger training, Dave mixed rookies with veterans for a 30-day to two-month mission.

Inside Burma's heartless, hellish war zone, we were all the same. Like the people we cared for, Rangers wrestled with hatred, rage, abandonment, loss, abuse and hopelessness.

An underlying objective anchored Dave and his core of leaders: to help every Ranger, resistance soldier and IDP realize their need for Jesus whom he served. Dave never tolerated anyone belittling an FBR member's religion or culture, but attitudes within the FBR reflected Christian principles.

All missions were bathed in prayer to God through Jesus Christ. As we experienced miracles and answers to our prayers offered in the name of Jesus, many of us dedicated our lives to serve our people as passionate soldiers of love and peace.

Seeing results of the savagery of the Burma Army overwhelmed us at times — but working on the frontlines changed us. Rather than hate the "tools" in the hands of pure evil, we focused on overcoming evil with good.

Our mission statement grew into a creed that describes our Commander's (God's) Intent:

To bring help, hope and love to people of all faiths and ethnicities in the war zones of Burma, to shine a light on the actions of the dictators' army, to stand with the oppressed and to support leaders and organizations committed to liberty, justice and service.

RANGERS IN THE GAP

Dave harnessed my battlefield experience from the start. In bamboo shelters, rookie medics crowded around me as I taught them to sterilize instruments in a rice cooker and also primitive methods of stitching up wounds. We simulated delivering babies (lots of laughter here), and I instructed basic first aid, including how to stanch a stubborn, pumping artery (most often a result of stepping on a landmine).

What I could not pass on to my hopeful students was how to block out the smell of gangrenous flesh or ignore screams as they probed their patients' wounds for shrapnel with forceps. Bullets might be piercing the flimsy bamboo walls of the very hut where they operated, and I prayed for my students to acquire a medic's nerve.

In time, we built permanent training centers in North Karen State, South Karen State, Shan State and in a neighboring country. In addition, we held special medical and logistics training camps wherever pro-democracy groups asked us to come.

෩෩෩෩

Burma's vast frontier borders five nations: Bangladesh, India, China, Laos and Thailand, and within it, a horseshoe of mountain ranges sculpt a formidable barrier to travel. Three seasons dominate the country: hot (March to May), rainy monsoon (May to October) and cold (November to February).

In 2001, our team searched out IDPs in the Karenni

State where the Tatmadaw had laid waste to village after village. Bodies lay in rice paddies where soldiers had beaten fathers to death.

Small groups of IDPs shuffled between burnt villages like zombies, hollow-eyed, with no more tears to cry. Many were Christians in the area, and we were surprised to find the church still standing. It had been looted and became a signpost of terror for the believers.

The year "2001" had been scraped into a wall along with the words: "We will scatter you!"

Immediately, our team went to work gathering IDPs from their jungle warrens. We set up a medical clinic, and our lead pastor began handing out hymn books and Bibles to church leaders who came when they heard we were in the area.

"Go take a bath. Get clean, and don't walk around downhearted. God loves you, and you must move on with your lives." The words came from our hearts. We understood their pain. We had been IDPs, too.

But one Karenni pastor trampled evil like dust. He wore a bright red tunic and clamped Dave with a little bear-cub hug. The pastor's smile lifted our spirits at once. His village had just been burned, and Dave asked him, "How can you smile? You were almost caught by the Tatmadaw!"

"I smile because Jesus is with me, and I am not afraid! They can kill my body, destroy my village and burn down my church, but they can't kill my soul. It belongs to Jesus, so that's why I smile!"

I felt a lump in my throat as Dave asked, "And why are you so dressed up?"

"Don't you know? It's Sunday!"

My Desolate Dooplaya

By 2002, FBR had sent teams on more than 40 missions, each group usually consisting of videographers, medics, radio operators, porters and pastors. Our teams had rushed to hotspots to help IDPs in districts in the Karenni State, Shan State and often in the Karen State — but never around my home district of Dooplaya.

I pushed the idea to mount a mission there after Karen leaders discussed the growing number of terrorized IDPs in the Dooplaya District. Where I had grown up, 5,000 Karens were running for their lives or had been herded into disease-ridden relocation camps. The foul stench of burning bamboo still clung to Tatmadaw uniforms after torching hundreds of homes, and at least one mass execution had occurred — leaving 12 people dead, mostly children.

Dave looked unusually solemn while our core team discussed logistics.

"Along with patches of jungle, there are also miles of rice fields — nowhere to hide. Thousands of Burmese soldiers bivouac in villages, and spies for the Tatmadaw are as thick as flies."

It was all true. Two local factions had joined the Tatmadaw, calling themselves the Democratic Karen

Buddhist Army and the Karen Peace Army. I called them *opportunists* and *traitors.*

"Let's pray," Dave said, and we formed a tight circle of faith.

We would leave the next week.

A security team of Karen soldiers met us at a rendezvous, as well as several porters we paid to accompany us, but already our mission felt tainted. Two KNLA men in our security detail had been scouting five miles ahead of our group and were surprised by the Tatmadaw.

According to a villager who ran to warn us, one soldier was dead. The other suffered a compound fracture from a bullet in the leg.

"Burma officers are torturing him," the quaking villager whispered.

Would he reveal the Free Burma Rangers' proposed route to Dooplaya?

Dave looked even more dubious about the trip. He worried that he might be a magnet for trouble — he couldn't hide his white skin very well, and the SPDC had lately asked a neighboring government to eject the "terrorist" Dave Eubank, as a diplomatic gesture.

Any Tatmadaw officer in Burma would have loved to pose with Dave's head on a pole for their propaganda photographer. Dave finally called his prayer partner, Karen, on the satellite phone — and he had his answer. The people of Dooplaya had requested help, and he felt motivated to go. Karen had peace about the mission, and her words helped him decide. We *all* would go to Dooplaya.

In Karen State, no one asked why we chopped through brambles and thorns instead of tramping down easier packed trails. According to our intelligence, 3,000 Burma soldiers camped strategically along our former route. As we arrived at the village of Mon, we received a tentative welcome and didn't stay long. We met with pastors and departed to sleep far from the village in the jungle.

Our radio suddenly crackled and sputtered as we ate our cold meals that night. We intercepted the Tatmadaw message: "A foreigner and Karen soldiers are coming ..."

"So, who do you think the spy was in Mon?" I laughed. No one had any idea.

My desolate Dooplaya.

"Yea, though I walk through the valley of the shadow of death ..." I recited Psalm 23 to myself, awestruck.

This was my homeland — stolen from my people. We found no animals and no fruit in the orchards. No rice waved green in the fields anymore. A year before, hundreds of people fled south when the Burma Army marched through. Then the Army returned to exterminate or herd the diehard farmers into special villages controlled by the soldiers. Thousands in the Dooplaya region now subsisted on jungle fruit and grew root crops and rice in shared gardens. They would rather die in the jungle than live in the squalid relocation camps.

When we found these courageous IDPs, they wept for joy.

LOVE NEVER WASTED

"We *knew* that God hadn't forgotten us!"

Our meager supplies of food were mere tokens and lasted but a few days. Our gifts of new clothing replaced their tattered, soiled sarongs and tunics, once crimson and sparkling white. To the Asian mind, a gift is given as a sincere offering of respect and love. Children inched from behind their tearful mothers as we spread toys, such as dolls and plastic cars, on bamboo mats.

"I'm Eliya! What is your name?"

I tossed a ball in the air and caught it behind my back a few times before handing it to a shy boy with eyes infected and swollen from insect bites. I remembered him later and treated him, along with hundreds of other gaunt, desperate countrymen and women.

Teachers had escaped their villages, leaving classrooms full of teaching aids behind. Now they huddled with parents and talked excitedly about building a hidden school in the area. Our team unpacked schoolbooks, tape recorders, cassettes and batteries. We taught them how to use solar panels so that kids could study in dimly lit huts at night.

We barely touched the immense physical needs of families surviving with handmade gardening tools, machetes for defense and no hope of rescue. But our love saturated them. We mingled, hugged, sang, ate and played together.

For years, we had trespassed Burma's corrupt powers to learn what the ethnic minorities on the frontiers needed most. Now we understood that the greatest relief we could offer was *intangible* and borne of hard-won experience. Free Burma Rangers were in the business of nurturing souls, and God's love nourished the heart long after the toys were lost and the rice we brought was gone.

Our FBR pastors reminded the Christians among the IDPs to pray to Jesus for daily inspiration and support. God loved everyone, no matter what religion, culture or political persuasion, and this included the Tatmadaw who hated them. To receive the peace of God, the Christians must forgive their enemies.

On the back of our olive-green t-shirts (we handed them out by the hundreds), our FBR motto read:

Love each other. Unite and work for freedom, justice and peace. Forgive and don't hate each other. Pray with faith. Act with courage. NEVER SURRENDER.

Around campfires or under thatched roofs in pouring rain, we shared this inspired truth that gave the Free Burma Rangers courage to stay in the battle. We knew that God would secure our destinies in heaven when we died. In return, we served him fully in this life — whatever the cost.

"Eliya! Play for us!" No matter how sore my fingers were, I strummed songs on my guitar for my IDP children while everyone sang.

I pulled teeth and drilled to fill cavities. Other medics and I treated respiratory diseases and supplied medicine for malaria, the deadly scourge of the jungle.

We offered how-to demonstrations in hygiene, like brushing teeth and sanitation. I conducted first-aid classes and lessons on basic anatomy and fundamental triage. Gunshot wounds often healed over pockets of infection, and I reopened them to kill pathogens. I could only sterilize and re-bandage stumps of arms or legs lost in landmine explosions. From our base of operation, word spread, and hundreds of IDPs from different hide sites came to be encouraged and medically treated — until all our support gifts were finally depleted.

"Are those meant for us?" Dave asked me as about 30 of us crouched in a thick copse of leafy bamboo. Dull mortar thuds and cracks from nearly a mile away kept us from moving to the next hide site.

Twenty members of our team were Karen security soldiers, and their leader explained, "The Tatmadaw is shelling a village. The people returned to live there without permission, and they don't like that."

We were involved only once in a firefight in Dooplaya. It happened while we were treating about 800 people at one of our jungle clinics. Our Karen soldiers repelled a battalion as they measured our defensive strength. We buried one security soldier, and a bullet raked open another man's face. We prayed with him before sending two carriers to see that he arrived at a hospital several days' journey south. We sent a note with them to our families that we were still safe.

Whenever we approached a relocation camp, we respectfully spoke to a headman before coming inside with our FBR crew. As tacit prisoners, they feared retribution if officers discovered we had given them food. At one of these camps, three of us were invited inside: our pastor, a photographer and myself, the medic.

The casualties included a 12-year-old boy we called Wilbur, whom I treated for a bullet wound. He was the lone survivor of the mass execution of the 12 Dooplaya villagers a month earlier. Machine-gun bullets had killed his grandmother, and she fell across Wilbur with a smother of dead bodies. Wilbur lay still until the executioners had gone, then he crawled to the road and walked for three days to this relocation site.

Wilbur's grandmother had been taking him to what she hoped would be a safer location when the Tatmadaw trackers found them. IDPs living at relocation camps never dared leave without written permission. This officer had made an example of his contrary captives.

I redressed Wilbur's wound, seeing a reflection of myself in his angry eyes. But I had been miraculously changed in my heart to forgive — and if God could transform *me*, he could give peace to *anyone* in Burma, including Wilbur. We prayed with the boy, gave him some money and quietly left the relocation site.

Acts of Love

Our Rangers found 12 fresh graves outside the village, not far from another group of exhausted, malaria-wracked IDPs. These 96 men, women and small children were on the way to a refugee camp, too. They had escaped from a relocation camp whose overlord would hunt them to hell and back to save face.

For seven days, they had been walking and hiding, and five weary Karen soldiers served as their guides.

We prayed with the 96 IDPs and the soldiers, cutting short our original mission in Dooplaya. We combined our 20 Karen soldiers and nine Free Burma Rangers with their company.

"Looks like we have our work cut out for us," I said, laughing, and Dave nodded.

"Acts of love are never wasted," he said, smiling.

I broke out my mobile pharmacy and began examining the weakest of our Burma nomads. I loved my job. And we all loved our precious IDPs — *every single one.*

But can these people move any slower?

One woman had given birth just before her escape from the relocation camp. She clutched a newborn to her breast, and we prayed he would survive. Another woman shuffled at the back of our formation, eight months pregnant, but smiling every mile.

We carried toddlers on our shoulders along with packs. Thin, weary preadolescents trudged after their mothers, silent but for deep coughs from lung ailments. The elderly men and women focused downward, willing their feet to move — one foot, then the next.

Our Karen guides chopped a trail through tangled bamboo, thorn brush and tall sawgrass. Gray mud sucked at sandals and boots, while snakes slithered patterns around our legs. Legions of mosquitoes clouded our vision. The nearly impassable swampland tortured mind and body, but easier paths led to much worse suffering.

Our radioman picked up military transmissions from behind, to either side and in front of us. The Burma Army seemed to be patiently drawing a net closed around us.

After our night hikes, we made cold camps on the brushy hills that separated swampy sections of coagulum.

While our weary company rested, the Free Burma Rangers visited two villages that had been burned to the ground weeks before. Villagers still foraged there, but their hearts were broken.

Christians had been rounded up and locked in their church for days. They heard their pastors and elders being tortured outside.

When the Burma Army left, they reportedly took the pastors to the infamous Kya In Seik Gyi prison.

Before we resumed our journey, we interviewed everyone, photographed the charred remains of the village and gave money to help the pastors' families.

About five days from our destination, nearly all of our feet and toes showed signs of jungle rot — a fungus infection like athlete's foot, times 10. Our indirect but safest route led through rivers, over mountains 2,000 feet high, then to sea level and again into more jungle and swamps.

One evening our main body caught up with the Karen guides who were resting at an obvious fork in the trail, and our charges flopped down behind us like tired lambs. One fork, a shorter route, included about five hours of traveling through rice fields, open to mortar fire if a battalion commander spotted us. This tempting approach put us within a day's hard walk across a border to safety.

But our radioman had snatched chatter from our pursuers. One commander with 200 soldiers stood in our path — *somewhere.* Three other Tatmadaw battalions boxed us in on our other three sides.

"It's safest to take the long way — to curl around the end of the battalion and sneak past, but this means five days total travel," our Karen leader said.

"We eat our last rations tonight, Dave," I reported.

We glanced back at the IDPs, now on their feet and building shelters for the night. It began pouring buckets of rain again, like it did every night during the Burma rainy season.

"We'll lose some of the kids, if we go the long way. But we can get most of the people through," the Karen leader continued in low tones. No one wanted to admit it — but that was reality.

"Let's pray," Dave said, kneeling, and we joined him, earnestly asking God for guidance.

Seconds after praying, we had consensus. We chose the longer, safer route.

Who is that?

A peculiar-looking elderly Karen man followed one of our security soldiers as he pushed toward us through a bamboo thicket. Rainwater drizzled down the man's brown, bald head.

A spy?

The old fellow's jutting jaw had obviously been set crooked after a break, and though hunched over, his bowlegs moved crablike with amazing agility.

I noticed rifle barrels drifting his direction until a Karen soldier identified him as a personal friend, a resistance fighter and a headman for a local village. Thinking him mad, the Burma Army had left him alone to wander about the countryside on his little horse.

"I have been trying to find you," Crabman said. "I know where the Burma Army is camped tonight — you need to go *that* way!"

He pointed a finger in the direction of our prayerfully rejected, quicker path to the border.

"Much open ground, but the Tatmadaw won't expect you to use a direct route."

All of us stood silent, assessing his words.

"The commander has moved his battalion *here.*" He drew a map in the muddy earth, marking exactly a point on our longer path that we planned to travel. "Take the easier way, and you'll be across the border in a day!"

That guy seemed like an angel! I thought, after he disappeared into the bamboo again.

According to our prayers for guidance, our consensus changed on a dime. We spent a final tense night bedded down, wide awake before our planned departure at 2 a.m. Fear hung thick, like humidity upon the flesh. Karen soldiers stood guard at the perimeter of the camp, and I rose to join FBR and KNLA leaders whispering tense exchanges about the next few hours.

A song suddenly rose in my heart. I bent into the grim circle of leaders, gently "strumming" my M-16, and singing quietly:

"Don't worry about tomorrow, it's really a good day today!
Jesus is right beside you to guide you all the way.
Have faith, hope and love — that is how to live.
And how do I know this truth? The Bible tells me so!"

I left the men chuckling and moved to the families huddled together. I encouraged them softly with words like: "Don't worry! Jesus is here!" and "God will get you to freedom! Be strong! Don't give up!"

In the darkness, I felt them smiling back at me, receiving my gift of love. The pall of fear in the camp lifted as if a refreshing breeze blew it away.

At 2 a.m., Dave and I roused our travelers from their leafy burrows, and we gathered to pray. We gave each adult a candle.

Free Burma Rangers, 96 IDPs and our brave Karen soldiers left our bivouac walking single-file with lighted wicks. We stayed in the jungle as long as we could, until breaking into the great expanse of uncovered rice fields.

"Lights out," we whispered to one another.

Along with the Karen point soldiers, Dave and I scouted ahead to guide our group past Tatmadaw units.

The Karen guerrillas set up a mobile base ahead of us, and a radioman intercepted all communications between Burma Army battalions.

Runners relayed messages back to us as we pressed the IDPs, "Keep moving! Good! Can I carry your little girl? Come on, Grandmother! We love you! We're almost home!"

One time we all stopped dead, lying flat on the ground, praying that our children would be silent. A small unit of men marched across our path 100 yards in front of us. When they had passed, Dave led the way forward until a Karen soldier huffed up to tell him that the commander and his 200 Tatmadaw soldiers had dug in to "repel" us.

What?

"They think that we are KNLA soldiers, heavily armed and coming to attack *them*!" he said breathlessly.

Dave and I stared at each other in disbelief. "Eliya, if they stay put, we can arc around them! We're only a few hours from the border!"

But a worrisome communiqué followed.

SPDC headquarters berated the commander: "NO! These are the escapees from Dooplaya! A bunch of Free Burma Rangers and old people. And children! You have 200 men. Move in! Move in!"

We intercepted one last dispatch before we left the 200 Tatmadaw soldiers in our muddy wake — from a Tatmadaw officer ravaged by a jungle fever.

The officer radioed his headquarters, "I cannot move in. I am too sick to command and bedridden in my tent."

LOVE NEVER WASTED

Hunger played with our minds as we lovingly pushed our IDPs toward freedom. We crossed rivers and climbed rocky hills. Bare feet bled, but we dared not stop except for short, regimented periods as we waited for reports from scouts. I medically treated whomever I could, in the time I had, praying that we might not lose a single child or elder.

No one complained. No one spoke aloud for miles.

After hours of agony on trails without protective cover, Dave gathered everyone into a tight circle and told them, "You're free. God has led us safely out of Burma."

We continued to a welcoming village, where we celebrated God's goodness and feasted on rice and chicken soup. Children suddenly acted like children again. Grandfathers and grandmothers laughed together, and our one pregnant mother looked forward to delivering her baby without fear.

ॐॐॐ

Cat and I live in a rural community in a country neighboring Burma. We had one child when I met Dave in 1997. Now we have four. We named our daughter Eubank Sam Samson. Dave's son is named Peter Eliya Eubank.

Dave and I still travel deep into Burma with other FBR members to help our people, but as I grow older, my role as chief medic for the Free Burma Rangers is marching into new territory.

I have flown to Washington, D.C., to testify about the atrocities committed by the Burma Army. I represented our Karen people, asking America and other nations for help in uniting Burma as a peaceful, democratic nation.

I administer the training program for our medics who have provided treatments and relief on more than 800 missions. I also have designed and built a medical and surgical clinic in a neighboring country.

I will always be "Wild Uncle Eliya" to Sahale, Suuzanne and Peter, and often Dave and I talk about the future. What if Dave and Karen lost the ability to work in Burma? What would happen to the Free Burma Rangers?

I tell Dave, "You are working for God, and he will use you anywhere. You have helped us very much already.

"We will carry on God's work in Burma. Our Rangers have good leaders now, like Doh Say, Ka Paw Say, Saw Sun and Sai Nawng — and great Karen warriors like me!

"God holds the reins of all nations. Don't worry about tomorrow."

CHAPTER 4
GEM OF DESTINY
SAI NAWNG'S STORY

*"God, I like this work with the Free Burma Rangers.
I want to stay with them for a long time.
If you are really God — make it happen."*
Sai Nawng — Shan State Team Coordinator,
Free Burma Rangers

Burma Army SOP:
Torture to Extract Intel

Guerrilla fighters led our team to IDP hide sites. My communications gear stored intelligence about our web of secret trails. I carried a satellite transceiver for sending e-mails, a handheld GPS, radio and video camera.

If I was taken alive, the Tatmadaw officer would toast his excellent karma while his soldiers sharpened stalks of bamboo. I would tell him that our Rangers' mission is: "To provide hope, help and love to internally displaced people inside Burma, regardless of ethnicity or religion." And he would laugh.

In village after village, our Free Burma Rangers team had filmed glassy-eyed people culling through charred remains of their homes. Our camera stored a full month of interviews with rape and torture victims. We documented names and villages of family members abused and/or executed — as well as the perpetrators' units and acting officers, when available.

After recording events on our Shan State mission, Free Burma Rangers would return to headquarters to broadcast our field reports, pictures, maps and interviews to thousands of supporters and media outlets around the world. We desperately needed volunteer workers and financial aid to bring relief to forgotten families in my Shan State.

But is telling the world the truth about my homeland worth dying for?

The question never leaves the mind of an ethnic Free Burma Ranger, no matter what his religion or culture.

ༀༀༀ

Our host was the headman (mayor) of the only village within several miles of us that was powered by a water-generated electrical plant. It was almost dark when he climbed his stairs after tending opium fields and offered us tea.

My fellow Ranger and friend, Yod, stood vigil at the open door. Yod was a videographer trained by the Free Burma Rangers to chronicle stories of internally displaced people. An armed SSA soldier had accompanied Yod and me to the village, and he squatted with his rifle in the shadows outside the headman's home.

GEM OF DESTINY

Our 30 Free Burma Rangers had visited seven village regions in the prior month, medically treating and encouraging hundreds of homeless Shan State IDPs. Yod and I fidgeted nervously, anxious to rejoin our FBR team members who were concealed a couple miles away in a cold jungle camp. Tatmadaw soldiers were tracking us, but we had no idea exactly how close they were.

A cornerstone of every Free Burma Rangers mission is communication. Above the din of birds, insects and monkeys, our radio waves carry warnings and data that save lives. But, on this occasion, heavy cloud cover had blanketed the sun for days, preventing us from solar charging our vital equipment.

Inside the headman's house, I sat cross-legged on a bamboo mat with camera, radio and satellite transceiver batteries plugged into electrical outlets, waiting for red lights to stop winking at me.

"Sai Nawng — you hear that?" Yod asked me.

Village dogs barked frantically outside. I sensed that something was wrong, but the headman brushed off my concern.

"Farmers are returning home from their fields, that's all."

A man outside crossed a shaft of window light, and I rose to my feet. It was our Shan security man. I glimpsed a blur of figures with rifles and canvas military hats outside, milling some distance away. We were likely cut off from the trail back to camp.

"Yod. Let's go."

We scooped up commo gear, stuffing some of it into my pack, and quietly stepped outdoors into near-darkness.

Our Shan security man moved quickly away, but Yod stopped. "The camera," he whispered. "I forgot it."

My friend disappeared for mere seconds and reappeared.

As our eyes adjusted to the darkness, more figures emerged from the shadows. A full Tatmadaw battalion would follow.

"Give me your gear! Run!" I said.

We bolted toward the jungle, and suddenly a voice screamed, not a dozen feet behind us.

"Stop! Don't move!"

With Yod's camera still in my hands and my pack full of communications gear, I knew what lay in store if I was captured. I breathed a prayer and sprinted toward the jungle.

Obsession

The expression on the Buddha's gold-plated face never changed, no matter how passionately I chanted before his image. Buddha just seemed to ignore me.

My brother, my two sisters and I grew up in a village several miles from where my grandparents lived, and my father worked from dawn to dusk on his small farm. Under a grass-thatched roof, our family lived in two bamboo rooms: one for cooking and eating, and one for sleeping. My mother kneaded and cooked rice noodles to sell from her shop in front of our house, but we seldom had enough rice or chicken to satisfy our own bellies.

I attended a primary school near our tiny village until I was 7. After that, my father sent me to live with my grandparents in Taunggyi, the capitol of the Shan State. My family enrolled me in a Burman government school there.

Grandfather was a Buddhist abbot at a monastery in Taunggyi. Taunggyi is the headquarters for the Eastern Command of the Tatmadaw, and when I was a child, my Shan family and friends accepted Burma Army soldiers as part of our community. The soldiers represented the law of the land, and boys were often conscripted into their ranks to help hunt down the pro-democracy resistance fighters based in rural Shan villages.

Growing up, my best friends were the monks who padded in and out of the temple monastery next door to my grandfather's home. I learned Theravada Buddhist chants in Pali (an ancient language of India), and Grandfather trained me to handle inevitable suffering in my life with meditation and spiritual disciplines. I even spent a month as a novice monk.

But I never followed in Grandfather's quiet footsteps. He might have been disappointed in me, except that he believed in karma, that my choices were determined by past lifetimes. The "being" I had been in a previous life determined the kind of man I would someday become.

As for my secular education, my school taught me that our Shan State was part of a wonderful union of Burma states. Our benevolent military leaders were Bamars, the ethnic majority and ruling class of Burma, who kept us safe from terrorists and political insurgents.

One day in 1988, when I was 14, our government ordered all schools in Burma closed. Thousands of students, monks, business people, farmers and even children gathered in the streets of Burma's larger cities to demand national elections. Citizens demanded a new multiparty government, rather than one-party Bamar military rule.

It took a month for our military leaders to crush this democracy movement and scatter the protestors. Our great and powerful rulers used the crisis to reorganize our government, calling it the State Law and Order Restoration Council (SLORC), and they renamed our country Myanmar.

After the '88 democracy uprising bled away, the SLORC ordered the doors to all schools and universities locked tight for two years. I stayed with my grandparents for a time, then moved back home to help my father on his rice farm. I never went back to school.

Is this why Sai Nawng was born? To swat flies off the rump of an ox?

As a solitary, brooding teenager, I contemplated my pathetic vocation. Father owned a single stubborn water buffalo, and it was my job to graze her in fields to keep her sleek and well-fed for plowing. My karma seemed tied to this beast, and I yearned to cut the rope!

GEM OF DESTINY

On hot evenings, my mind wandered to the gem mines of Mong Hsu. Padamyas (rubies) glittered in my head. Alluring. Seductive. A single exquisite gem could transform my destiny. Riches would bring me a beautiful wife, plenty of rice for my family and, above all, respect from my community.

After three restless years of goading and chasing my father's cultivating beast, I left the farm and hiked into the mountains of Mong Hsu, some of the richest gem-bearing grounds on earth. Today multi-million-dollar open-pit mining companies chew up our Shan landscape. But in the early '90s, iron teeth and diesel engines were few in number. Hundreds of prospectors, like me, honeycombed the mountains with picks and shovels.

I gambled away three years of my life, burrowing into holes seven days a week to find the ruby that would change my life. I only found enough poor-quality gemstones to lure me deeper into my obsession — *until one morning ...*

A magnificent ruby lodged in the wire mesh of my sifting bucket! It glittered like a sparkling drop of pigeon's blood, and I gawked like a schoolboy, glancing around warily. I wrapped the gem in a piece of cloth and crammed it into my pocket.

I lit candles of thanksgiving before Grandfather's golden Buddha in Taunggyi, but the image still wore the same empty expression — not happy for me or sad. Just *uninterested.*

I sold my crimson ruby, and suddenly everyone in my

village wanted to be the clever gem miner's best friend. Women loved me, and my community praised my ingenuity. I bought a house near my family and dressed in a jaunty striped longyi (waist-to-ankle attire) and fine sandals. I purchased a sleek new water buffalo to work in Father's rice fields and purchased a milk cow for our family.

I drove through the streets on a shiny black motorcycle, feeling like Buddha's favored child, while a relentless lust for more wealth pursued me.

"Let's go into business!" I said. "We will be gem dealers!"

Some in my family joined me in my risky venture, while larger mining companies crowded into the Shan State. The Tatmadaw seized control of the best gem-producing regions, and like a slow hemorrhage, my obsession for wealth drained every Kyat from my bank account. I sold my motorcycle, then the cow and finally the family water buffalo — to pay off debts.

Suddenly no one wanted me around anymore. I packed up my evil karma and hitched a ride out of Burma, searching for some reason to keep on living.

In a neighboring country, I lived in constant fear of arrest by the local police as I worked without a permit. While pumping fuel for customers at a gas station, I sifted through my past, wondering again why I was ever born.

Suddenly, the gem of a scheme overwhelmed my troubled mind. *Why couldn't I unearth my good luck again — in a Mong Hsu cave?*

GEM OF DESTINY

I saved up money and traveled back to the Shan State, begging Buddha or karma or *someone* to help me find a ruby that would give my life meaning.

Circle of Pain

I found work with a foreign mining company, but on days off, I stole away to hunt gems in mines owned by the Wa State Army. My obsession for wealth only drove me deeper into a sullen, bitter despair.

One night I tripped down a hill to a creek with a promising bucket of gravel, breathing a Pali chant for luck, and knowing my fate if Wa soldiers spotted me. But it was worth the risk — one padamya could change my karma forever.

With bruised and bleeding hands, I held a candle close, squinting at shiny pebbles in the flickering light, but ...

Nothing. They were all worthless — *like me.*

Squatting alone in the darkness, covered in muck, the flame of my blind ambition flickered out. Years of my life had fallen away, like byon through wire mesh.

My father was happy to have me home, and I lasted only three months tending his cultivating equipment again. No woman that I knew was interested in starting a life with me. I owned nothing and carried buckets of bitterness within my soul. All hope of reclaiming respect in my community I left in the caves of Mong Hsu.

I decided to leave Burma and return to a region where

I could hold my head up because no one knew about my failures. In the neighboring country where I had worked before, the fuel company bribed officials so that I could pump gas again.

I met a young woman whose parents also lived in my Taunggyi District in Burma, and we married. She convinced me to return to our Shan community to work for her father, who owned several water buffalo and even a farm tractor!

With our precious new son, we settled near her father's fertile rice fields, not far from my own family that I had shamefully left behind.

For the first few months in Taunggyi, I ignored stories about the Burma government tightening its stranglehold upon our Shan culture. I tried to stay neutral, but in our village, groups of Burma Army bullies were strutting like peacocks on our streets.

"Pigs. Shan are *lower* than pigs!"

A Tatmadaw soldier stood smirking a challenge in my grandfather's Shan Buddhist temple. He was flanked by several other ethnic Burmans, and a flash of rage at his disrespect flooded my chest. I slammed my fist into the soldier's jaw and followed with a kick. Other Shan worshipers helped me teach the Burmans a lesson, and we spilled into the street.

A ring of armed Tatmadaw soldiers closed in on the last three of us fighting outside our temple, and their rifle butts pounded us to the dirt. The soldiers marched us to jail, and during my first night behind bars, we three Shan prisoners stood back to back, fighting off other jailed Burmans.

Inmates in Burma jails never receive food or bedding, except from families or friends, and the next day I expected my wife or father-in-law to visit me. I expected my family to offer the police the customary bribe to free me, but no one came. Three days passed, and I grew more disheartened as I watched scolding wives lead fellow prisoners away from our stinking cell.

"What will it take for me to get out of here?" I finally asked a guard.

He named his price.

"Done! Let me out, and I'll go home and get it."

The guard opened my cell.

How could my karma curdle like sour milk so soon?

My fight at Grandfather's temple was nothing compared to the verbal melee with my in-laws. They berated me and called me a gangster. They poisoned my wife's heart with lies, and when I asked for help to pay the police bribe, they refused. My father-in-law fired me outright.

I searched my wife's face, my last hope, but she shook her head.

"Sai Nawng, this is not your home anymore." I reached toward my firstborn son in her arms, and she jerked him away. "You don't have a child anymore, Sai Nawng. Or a wife. Get your things and get out."

Stunned and dejected, I headed for a local pawn broker

to hock my few possessions. I paid the police bribe, then walked to my brother's house. It wasn't easy asking my successful sibling for a place to stay. He lived on his farm outside of Taunggyi, and my elderly parents lived nearby.

My brother distilled rice liquor, and over time, I became his best customer. My family left me alone to stagger around in confusion, and I fell in with a gang of opium-sodden ne'er-do-wells who pilfered businesses in the area.

Ranger Rising

I blamed the Tatmadaw for destroying my future. My one taste of jail had soured me on spending time in prison, so I left my circle of thieving friends — and joined the Shan State Army.

The SSA soldiers were pro-democracy fighters who trained in remote jungle camps. I fell in with hundreds of angry, disillusioned Shan men and women just like me.

We recruits trained with wooden rifle replicas, and I learned guerrilla tactics to plague Tatmadaw battalions. I relearned the history of Burma from the perspective of Shan freedom fighters, and their officers turned me into a disciplined soldier.

My first year passed without seeing action, then my commander gave me my first assignment, but I wasn't pleased.

"You will escort a group of relief workers called the Free Burma Rangers. Assist them in finding displaced villagers in the Karen State. The Rangers distribute food and medicine to the Karen people at hide sites."

Hide sites?

I had no idea that thousands of people barely survived in secret communities in my neighboring Karen State. They lived in the jungle like animals, hiding from the Tatmadaw who used them as beasts of burden for construction projects and farming.

On my first mission with the Free Burma Rangers, I identified with the despair these internally displaced people felt. Some hated the Burma Army as I did, and I listened to them unburden their souls to Rangers who recorded their stories.

At hide sites, FBR medics sewed up gunshot wounds and pulled rotten teeth. Rangers coaxed smiles from sickly children clinging to mothers. They sang songs with IDPs and ate their meals with them.

The Free Burma Rangers professed to be Burma's cry for justice to an uninformed world.

While working with them, a powerful, selfless energy seized me, too. In dripping tents swarming with mosquitoes, I helped set up video cameras or monitored radio transmissions. I stood guard at the perimeter of the medical clinics, and my efforts fulfilled me — in the same way my grandfather must have felt satisfied when he arranged candles and lotus flowers for a festival.

In the Karen State, my eyes were opened to a confusing paradox: Men of my own faith had joined a paramilitary unit called the Democratic Karen Buddhist

Army (DKBA) — and swore allegiance to the Tatmadaw! Bands of the DKBA bandits ambushed local pro-democracy groups and stripped villagers of their ability to survive, by stealing rice and livestock.

Among the Free Burma Rangers, only a few men carried weapons. Before the mission, our FBR leaders reinforced their credo to NEVER engage the Tatmadaw or the Buddhist bandits, unless protecting innocent villagers or themselves. Rangers were under orders to stand between IDP families and *all* dangers — whether they had defensive weapons or not. They were trained to lay down their lives to save the people.

As we hiked single-file along steep, narrow trails, we often intercepted radio chatter about the Rangers. Only with the help of the ill-equipped and undermanned Karen National Liberation Army (KNLA) guides, could we navigate the safest routes to avoid the Tatmadaw and find the jungle hide sites.

I carried a heavy pack full of medical supplics, slipping and sliding in mud, for a full month. After the Free Burma Rangers mission was completed, I rejoined my SSA unit, but a troubling question lingered in my mind.

What motivated these men and women to risk their lives for IDPs like they were beloved family members? I wondered at the *purpose* I saw in their weary smiles, and I envied them.

To utterly dispirit my Shan people, the Tatmadaw began using the same loot-and-burn tactics that crushed villagers in the Karen State. My commander called me to the frontlines to serve with my SSA brothers-in-arms, and it took several months before the Burma Army pulled back.

I was elated when I received my commander's new orders to train with the Free Burma Rangers. During my six-week course at their headquarters in the Karen State, I met the Rangers' founder, Dave Eubank, who helped me finally discover my gem in the sands of destiny.

For two years, I worked closely with FBR teams, while my kinship with Dave and the Rangers grew stronger. Without my knowledge, Dave marked me as a potential team leader for relief missions in the Shan State.

As a Buddhist SSA soldier in my early 30s, my mind hovered between two domains: one clouded by bitter karma, and the other illuminated by these Christians. Dave invited me to pledge my allegiance to Jesus — the one true God whom he said answered prayers — but I resisted. To me, god was an impersonal, universal "force" that Buddha taught us to harness for personal enlightenment. But to these Christians, God was a friend.

As we encountered people who experienced unimaginable heartache and physical suffering, the Christians offered hope to the IDPs. But I had little hope to offer them — because I believed that karma cast a shadow of fatalism upon the future.

In my grandfather's district of Taunggyi, artisans harvest lotus flowers from Inle Lake and extract fibers for weaving exquisite, colorful fabrics. Their textile artistry is unique to Taunggyi, a place where weavers turn lotus plants into shawls and scarves. Weavers collect 1,200 water-borne lotus flowers for a single scarf, and each one takes weeks to finish.

I had no idea that a master weaver spun events in my life — since the fabric appeared so ragged and incomplete. But, strand by delicate strand, God was personally handcrafting his purposes into my destiny.

Dave taught his Rangers that Jesus embodied *all* true enlightenment and that God loved everyone — including the Tatmadaw soldier. Working with Dave and the Free Burma Rangers began to fundamentally change my view of the world.

రిం రిం రిం

On groundbreaking Shan and Karen missions between 2005 and 2007, I served with Dave Eubank, and we became good friends. Often we marched through Tatmadaw crosshairs together while building a backbone network for harried villagers to receive supplies and medical help.

The Burma government's modus operandi has always been to sow panic in thousands of Shan villagers who flee to the jungle to survive. On one three-month mission near the Shan Districts of Mong Pan, Lang Kur, Mong Nai and Khun Hing, we documented 113 killings of civilians and 24 rapes and murders of women and girls by the Burma Army soldiers.

Of the 150,000 people living in these four districts, 45

percent had fled to neighboring countries. Thirty-five percent lived in government relocation camps (Army-controlled villages), and 15 percent hid in jungle communities.

We tried to locate massacre sites to identify the villagers' loved ones, but abandoned the effort due to Burma Army patrols. Many IDPs and villagers had been enslaved to work on castor oil farms or cut and haul teakwood. The Burma government clear-cut Shan timber reserves to trade hardwood for weaponry.

At each medical clinic, we treated malnutrition, dysentery, malaria, as well as neglected injuries caused by shrapnel and landmines. We cared for more than 7,800 IDPs and villagers. Shan families suffered severe psychological traumas and were haunted by memories:

- One 17-year-old girl was raped for two days by three Burma Army soldiers.
- A mother was raped and her children forced to watch. The FBR relief team counseled her 5- and 7-year-old daughters who also had been abused.
- FBR discreetly documented the names of victims, the horrific events and names of the deceased.
- Pa Kum Yi: Raped by 20 men, shot and thrown into a river.
- Lon Paw Ka: Impaled with a spear and placed over a fire pit. Burned to death by Burma soldiers.
- Nan Mon Kum: Raped by 27 men and injected with heroin. Killed by Burma Army soldiers.

- Sai Tak Lon: Captured while traveling to his farm. Shot and killed by Burma Army soldiers.
- Ka Ti Ya: One cow, seven buffalo, 40,000 Kyat stolen. Beaten to death by Burma Army soldiers.
- Pi Ti: 90,094 Kyat stolen. Nine cows. One ox cart and three buffalo. Killed by Burma Army soldiers.
- Two villagers escaped before a mass execution. Burma Army soldiers forced villagers to march into the jungle. Some of the women were raped before the bloodbath. The next day, families and mourners found 27 bodies.

Once, our team was cornered by the Tatmadaw at a ford where the Salween River ran high and wild due to heavy rains. Dave gathered us to pray, and I bowed my head, too, as a Buddhist who respected all religions. We escaped with our lives by quickly assembling bamboo carrier rafts and swimming alongside our supplies.

Many times on the trail we experienced concrete, unnatural outcomes in events when Dave prayed for our direction and safety. Over the years I found it more and more difficult to ignore this Jesus whose name FBR leaders invoked whenever we needed help.

"If You Are Really God"

Over time, a disapproving SSA commander decided to separate me from the influence of the Free Burma Rangers.

He ordered me far away for officer training in the Northern Shan State, but his efforts backfired.

During this six-month period while I trained, a serious fall paralyzed my legs. Helpless where I lay in my bunk, I desperately prayed to Jesus, like he understood my pain and had the ability to cure me. Dave and other Christians joined me in asking God to restore feeling and strength to my legs, and within a week, I regained full use of my limbs!

Not only did God prove himself to me during this trial, but my SSA officer training prepared me well for a permanent position as a leader with the Free Burma Rangers.

కాకాక

"Congratulations, Ranger."

Dave and I shook hands, and I felt honored that the FBR leadership considered me competent to oversee logistics for all Shan State conflict zones. With the consent of the SSA commanders, I accepted the position Dave offered, amazed that God was answering my *unspoken* heart's desire. I had been praying that God would give me a job with the Free Burma Rangers and keep me with them for a long time.

No matter our religious beliefs, FBR workers learn and follow unequivocal Christian principles to guide our decisions. Leaders who are Jesus followers gather Buddhists, Animists or Atheists into prayer circles when

Rangers or IDPs need help. Over time, no honest FBR worker can deny that God, whom our founders, Dave and Karen Eubank, serve, energizes and often rescues our teams.

After accepting the position as Shan State FBR coordinator, I spent time with Dave and his family, and Dave's father, Allan, further introduced me to the Son of the one true God, Jesus Christ. True enlightenment flooded my heart, and I hungered to know God better. Pastor and respected friend, Allan Eubank, baptized me as a Jesus follower. I was 35 years old.

This God was not like the ruthless karma-slinging force that I had begged for rubies. He was compassionate, kind and just. God had created all men and women to love him, but people, like me, demanded to rule themselves. Pain and suffering resulted from our rebellion, so to save us from an eternal judgment, Jesus lived as a human being to realize the depth of our traumas.

Then God sacrificed his Son, Jesus, to pay for our insurrection. Jesus opened wide the door for everyone — whether IDP or Burma Army soldier — to experience undeserved soul peace.

స్తాస్తాస్తా

When the soldier had screamed, "Stop! Don't move!" my friend Yod and I tried to quickly melt into the darkness. I lost track of Yod, but I knew that at least one soldier had me dead in his sights.

GEM OF DESTINY

Shots rang out, and the shock of a bullet from an MA-1 Burmese rifle jarred my spine. I tripped, rolling into a deep ditch. At the bottom, I lay stunned for a few seconds. Water in the ditch trickled around me, and I took the time to stuff the camera into my pack and check my back for a gaping hole. No blood gushed from a painful spot, but I had little time to feel relieved. Bullets began plopping in the mud around me. I squirmed like an eel along the ditch, away from the village. When I felt safe enough to stand to my feet, I ran.

That's when M-79 grenade launchers unloaded on my position. Only God could have saved me that night as explosions dogged my every step. The ditch petered out, and I crashed like a boar into thick bamboo and brambles, out of breath and high on adrenaline.

I soon realized that I was climbing a mountain. Shrouded in darkness, I zigged and zagged up the rocky hillside, relieved that grenade bursts fell farther behind me. I recognized longer-range mortar rounds detonating on my trail instead and hurried straight up the incline until I was out of their range, too.

After about an hour, I fell to my knees, winded and disoriented.

Trackers would spread out to find me. If only I could use my flashlight for a little while ...

But I didn't dare. I ran again, to the top of the mountain and down the other side, then up again. My boots left deep gouges in the mud for the Tatmadaw trackers to follow, then rain poured from a black canopy above me. It washed away my trail, but chilled me to the bone.

I tripped over rocks and through thickets until stumbling into a rocky gap in the mountainside. I briefly lit the interior of a cave and crawled deep inside, praying that the snakes and centipedes might let me share their space for a few hours.

Leaning my back against cold stone inside, my mind conjured up a younger man squirming into similar holes scraping for rubies — but the memory evaporated when I began to pray.

I imagined what the villagers might be suffering because they had harbored Free Burma Rangers. The Burma Army soldiers would dig out every pebble of information about us.

And where was Yod?

The GPS blinked 5 a.m. when I crawled from my hole in the ground. I peered down at the rising fog drifting above the village, now as silent as death. Then I stared into the dense jungle — where I had lost my FBR team and camp.

If BA soldiers glassed me from a distance, my rucksack would give me away, identifying me as important quarry. So I concealed my equipment carefully inside the cave to retrieve it later.

I hoped that I looked like a villager, and only the quiet squawk from my radio spoke otherwise. I discreetly marked waypoints on my GPS, moving down the mountain toward the village — exactly where I did *not* want to go. But I needed to cross a familiar trail to find my way back to the FBR camp.

On the valley floor, dogs were barking again — this time at me — so I skirted the village, hoping that the BA soldiers had left the area.

I hunkered in a bamboo thicket to study my GPS, but the readings appeared to be corrupted. It was as if someone had erased my waypoints and tracks back to our camp! Even worse, now my GPS was useless in finding the cave where I left the rucksack full of equipment.

By radio, I briefed our mission leaders back at camp, and they described a rocky cliff, from which I might gain my bearings — and they identified a trail below, leading to camp.

Climb again.

I stuffed my idle GPS in a pocket and trudged up, up to the rocky outcropping, then down the mountain again, hoping to find the trail the Rangers had described. Finally I resorted to hollering — and I heard faint voices from below me in the dripping tangle of green.

I bushwhacked my way down and, within minutes, stumbled into our camp, exhausted.

Our SSA security man, who had accompanied us to the headman's house, returned without Yod.

While I explained to leaders about our challenges the previous night, a rain-soaked villager came in, out of breath, flanked by an SSA soldier.

My good friend, Yod, was dead.

I hid my face in my hands as I listened.

"They shot him in the back! Then the soldiers searched him for a gun, to see if he was with the resistance, but they found nothing. If they had, they might have burnt our village!

"They shot another man in a ditch, too, but could not find him. He was wounded and ran away. He must have died in the jungle somewhere. They fired many mortars at him!"

The villager's face suddenly contorted with a painful memory. "The Tatmadaw … they beat our headman. They hit him with their rifles and pounded out his teeth."

I called Dave at headquarters to report the tragedy, and grief silently swept through our souls for a few seconds.

I could hear Dave take a deep breath. "Sai Nawng, you must find that equipment that you hid. We can't let the Burma Army get their hands on it!"

Together we petitioned God that he would help us find it. Our tech equipment was vital to traveling safely through hostile regions and necessary for documenting events. But without tracking coordinates stored in my GPS, I had no idea where the cave or equipment was. I spent the next day trying to retrace my steps, but failed time and again. We enlisted villagers and Shan soldiers to help us hunt, but the rocky mountain seemed to have swallowed up my pack. A miserable rainy dusk closed in, and I wearily knelt on a trail back to camp.

"God? What do I do? Keep searching or return empty-handed?"

I returned to camp, depressed. In my hammock, I wrestled with my failure. Recorded on the lost camera were hours of passionate, illuminating interviews and irreplaceable documentation. If the Tatmadaw found the computer to analyze, our logistical secrets and names of allies might be discovered. I prayed for mercy one last time before finally drifting off to sleep.

At 3 a.m., I awoke with a start, *knowing* that I must access my defective GPS again. By flashlight I studied a topo map, squinting at old GPS waypoints and jotting down notes. By 5:30 a.m., I alerted my SSA comrades that I remembered where the trail to the cave was.

Within 45 minutes, we found my cave and the equipment!

Yod is never far from my memory as I journey in his footsteps. Yod's sacrifice for his people fired a new intensity in my heart to love and serve people like he did. The words our FBR counselors speak to abused and homeless Christians in Burma give me peace when I think of Yod.

"This country is not our home. Life really begins when our days reach their end. Our citizenship is in heaven!"

Sometimes I remember lying in that muddy ditch, feeling for a gaping hole in my back. I believed that I was a dead man. But the soldier's bullet had lodged in a lead plate in the satellite transceiver inside my rucksack. Today a slight scar from fragments of the exploding satellite transceiver reminds me *who* is in charge of my destiny.

Good Life Boot Camp

"You're crazy, Sai Nawng!"

Most of my Buddhist family has disowned me because I am a Jesus follower.

"Why do you change your religion after being with those strangers? Go away! You can't share our rice!" they say.

But the same Jesus who transformed me from a greedy ruby miner to a Free Burma Ranger changes people around me.

My second wife, Loi, is a former Buddhist who found Jesus after we were married, and now my father is beginning to accept me as his son again!

Loi and I live as the only two Christians in our Buddhist community. From our home, I travel and work between the Free Burma Rangers headquarters in the Karen State and our training facilities in the Shan State. My job is equipping FBR leaders for the hard tasks of delivering relief to IDPs at hide sites or wherever they are enslaved by the Tatmadaw.

Serving in the Free Burma Rangers engages body, mind and spirit. At our training camps we simulate life-threatening conditions that Rangers typically confront in the Shan mountains, like disarming or moving landmines, swimming with loaded packs in bone-chilling rivers and rappelling off cliffs with soldiers in pursuit.

We replicate village massacres — complete with simulated mortar fire. We mentor our Rangers to reach deep for the willpower necessary to carry injured victims for miles to a clinic.

Every day, except Sundays, during our six-week FBR boot camp, we include two punishing physical training sessions, camp cleanup and seven hours of brainwork, like mapmaking and GPS instruction.

We evaluate new Rangers to find team leaders for future missions. ALL religious faiths are welcomed and encouraged to join the Free Burma Rangers. Our conspicuously Christian principles demand that we overcome ethnic prejudices, and our teamwork is crucial to every mission.

By graduation ceremony, our Shan Free Burma Ranger team members have learned basic medical skills, reporting, lifesaving, rappelling, swimming, counseling, photography, videography, mapping, land navigation, GPS and outreach to children.

Immediately after graduation, our leaders round up new Rangers and plan their first exciting mission. In 2012, we treated nearly 3,000 patients on just one four-month mission through the Shan State.

I remain cautiously optimistic about the latest cease-fire negotiations between some of Burma's ethnic states and the SPDC (State Peace and Development Council, formerly the SLORC), the ruling junta. But during this fragile semi-peacetime, we have watched the Burma Army resupplying and upgrading military camps, still using forced labor.

In the Kachin State, they have introduced helicopters

equipped with 105mm guns to ferry equipment to remote areas. At Tatmadaw camps in the Karen State, soldiers are constructing helipads for the first time.

Arbitrary arrests of accused pro-democracy individuals continue, and meaningful quantities of humanitarian relief are still blocked by the Burma Army.

In 2013, 47 Shan Rangers graduated from our Leadership and Relief Team Training, and we sent them to our southern border where clashes with the Burma Army continue, despite the negotiated cease-fire agreement.

ॐॐॐ

Overcome evil with good …

Our most powerful tool for shaping Burma's future was born on the frontlines of our civil war.

We call it the Good Life Club.

It happened when Free Burma Rangers co-founder Karen Eubank camped with other Rangers in a village under constant threat of attack. Children and mothers flocked to a theater of mercy — where they observed wounds being stitched or malaria diagnoses given. The IDP children were delighted to be distracted from the cares of daily survival.

Wherever Karen traveled, she longed for Burma's children to find the good life from God, in the midst of evil circumstances. Yet to help so many needy children seemed an impossible task. Building trust with such bruised and abused people *individually* took time that none of us had.

GEM OF DESTINY

Karen resolved to design an easy-to-follow child-evangelism curriculum for Rangers to teach within their relief programs. She developed fun and informal classes that included basic hygiene, anatomy and first aid, all wrapped into an entertaining message of love and hope.

Karen tailored her program to fit hide sites or village environments, and soon Rangers filled the jungle with singing and exciting Bible-based dramas. Rangers played games, performed skits and distributed gifts. To teach basic anatomy, we wore and handed out plastic aprons colorfully designed with major organs located in the appropriate places.

As our GLC program grew, we gave mothers and children gift packs supplied by churches and organizations filled with things like fingernail clippers, vitamins, combs, toothbrushes, toys, t-shirts, etc.

Our horse caravans packed in books and learning materials for the teachers to use in their school huts.

In time, child trauma counselors accompanied our teams to help victims of rape and other physical and psychological abuses cope with their memories.

Some of our Rangers are kitted out to be special uncles to our GLC children, like my good friend Doh Say. Together, Doh Say and I have survived Tatmadaw bullets. He is a living, breathing miracle, who should be dead, like me.

Doh Say is a man unencumbered by a permanent home or dreams of wealth, and he carries all that he owns in a single backpack.

RANGERS IN THE GAP

He is one of Free Burma Rangers' most beloved uncles and a respected Karenni freedom fighter. As I am in charge of the Shan State teams, Doh Say is responsible for all Ranger teams in the Karenni State — and he is also our Good Life Club coordinator for all of Burma.

CHAPTER 5
POWER IN SMILING EYES
DOH SAY'S STORY

"I will always try to find a way to help the oppressed."
Doh Say — Karenni State Team Coordinator,
Free Burma Rangers, Former Karenni
Director of Foreign Ministry

Warped Loyalties

I loved playing in the ore pits where my parents worked all day. Explosions growled in the belly of the mountains, but we miners' kids barely noticed. Dynamite shocked the Mawchi hills as often as dogs yapped at the pigs in our village.

It was dusk at the Mawchi mine, and my three older sisters gathered up my two little brothers and groused at me.

"Doh Say! We're going home now!"

I happily threw down my "machete" (a broken axe handle) and slid down a mound of dredge tailings. Mother's smile was as worn as her sandals. She came trudging toward us, and Father wasn't far behind. Gaunt and pale, he slapped his hat on a dirty thigh and hawked up mine dust.

Powder monkeys blasted the ore from the mountains. When Father wasn't shoring up mine shafts with timbers, he hauled carts of tin and tungsten ore to a sorting station. The ore was processed to make solder for electronic circuit boards for companies like Sony. Tungsten was used worldwide for filaments in light bulbs and in alloys to strengthen blade edges and drill tips.

In the '70s, no engineers "safety terraced" the ore pits of Mawchi, and every day that Father and Mother weren't buried alive or drowned in dredge holes was a *good* day.

The six of us kids scampered like dutiful brown ducklings behind my parents on the path to our bamboo home.

Oh, how I missed my brothers and sisters while I was away at school!

I lived with my well-off aunt and uncle at Loikaw, 96 miles away from Mawchi. At Loikaw, the capital of our Karenni State in Burma, I attended a government school after I turned 6 years old. When school let out for the summer, I seldom visited my family at home — but when I did, I cherished every minute!

On the footpath to our village, I glanced back fondly at broken buckets, rotting wooden troughs and tool handles scattered on alluvial piles. We wouldn't be meeting on our improvised playground tomorrow. Sunday was our day of rest, and my family attended the Baptist church in our village.

Two generations before I was born, Baptist missionaries arrived at our then-remote village and introduced my grandparents to Jesus. Since then, our family has called ourselves Christians. In Loikaw, my aunt (who loved me very much) and my uncle took me to a Baptist church, too — but they sometimes spoke ill of my father and mother.

"They don't take care of you children well, Doh Say. Your parents are tight-fisted and cheap! We don't respect them ..."

I had begged my father not to send me to live with relatives at Loikaw ...

In my formative years, my aunt and uncle nurtured seeds of bitterness against my father and mother. But how could I know that my father's lungs were weak from breathing mine fallout? He and my mother sometimes skipped meals to feed us. They worked in the mines to pay for my sister and me to go to school in the city. They prayed that we might find gainful, safe jobs and help our family someday.

And my parents *never* felt safe.

An ever-present fear of the Burma Army (under the rule of the Burma Socialist Program Party — the BSPP) wafted across the Mawchi Township like the odor of sulfur. Father even built a secret attic room in our home that we used when I was about 5 years old. I'll never forget the panic in his voice.

"Hurry. They're coming!"

My brothers and sisters, my mother and I scrambled through a hole in the ceiling, and we scrunched into a room barely big enough for *us*, let alone my father. The house was silent except for our breathing in the humid, stale air inside our oversized closet. When Father climbed in, too, it was stifling.

The Tatmadaw collected their quota of porters among our friends and neighbors and moved on to the next village. The Burma Army conscripted villagers to do "loh ah pay" (forced labor), like shouldering ammunition boxes or bags of rice. The porters walked in *front* of their battalions — and sometimes they detonated forgotten landmines soldiers had planted on the trails.

After the cries of protest finally stopped outside, we unfolded our stiff limbs and dropped into the main room of our house.

A breeze touched our sweaty necks and faces as we looked each other over. We had been miserable, angry and afraid — but at least we were *together.*

I come from a fiercely independent Karenni people whose traditions unite most of us —whether Animist, Buddhist or Christian. For centuries, we Karenni have shed blood to repel invaders who tried to dominate us. Usurpers clear-cut our teak forests, stripped our mineral resources and enslaved many of us.

Our homeland is hemmed in by the Karen State, Shan State and Thailand, and we still reject being included in the Union of Burma, at least until the junta is replaced by a democratically elected multiparty system of government.

We worked together with Great Britain to drive out Japanese troops from Burma during World War II, and the British awarded Karenni soldiers a shield to recognize their bravery and sacrifice. The inscription read: "We honor a nation who we did not colonize, and we'll remember them from sunset until sunrise."

Then the British left us to *defend* our sovereignty.

In 1947, we Karenni celebrated the New Year by hoisting our own flag at the Loikaw stadium, even as a new Burman-led government in Rangoon plotted to steal our independence.

Without our leaders' consent, a Burma military dictatorship incorporated our Karenni State into their "Union of Burma."

Karenni leaders sent a delegation to Rangoon to protest the imperialistic action, but our irresolute representatives (some say they were bribed) agreed to cooperate with the new Burma government.

The new Union of Burma sent military police to control demonstrations at Loikaw, and the following year a new and more resilient dictatorship took control of Burma. Their ruthless Tatmadaw immediately occupied our Karenni State.

In 1957, the Karenni National Progressive Party (KNPP) formed its own de facto governing body. The KNPP continues to recruit and deploy resistance soldiers to fight for our sovereignty as an independent nation. Our freedom fighters defend villages against the Burma Army and aid relief groups that help our people displaced by war.

RANGERS IN THE GAP

ॐ ॐ ॐ

The Union of Burma flag fluttered above the trembling girl as the seasoned bamboo cane struck her thighs for the 10th time. Like a shivering abacus, my mind configured every rule in our handbook as I watched. My Auntie had enrolled me in boarding school, and I planned to avoid any beatings with my unquestioning obedience.

At least, I started out that way ...

Teachers at my Burma government school insisted that I learn and communicate in the national tongue: Burmese. Members of the BSPP taught me informally that patriotic Karennis owed their allegiance to the government of Burma and that our enemy was the insurgencies, a rebel network whose members decapitated villagers and burned their homes!

In middle school, I was a model student — a good citizen of the Union — but by high school, I had changed.

An acute sense of abandonment darkened my thoughts, and I stopped visiting my family in Mawchi. Inner rage displaced my fear of caning, and any teacher who challenged me became my enemy. In subjects like English and even in my favorite class, mathematics, I lost interest and fell behind. Unable to catch up with the other students, I grew sullen, and my teachers were outraged at my disrespect.

A diploma was every student's ticket to a government-funded college education, but my grades were plummeting. In ninth grade, I stumbled off the academic path for which my parents sacrificed and quit school altogether. I spent a year wallowing in self-pity, trying to find work, before deciding to make one last stab at graduating from high school.

In the school office, I stood like I expected a caning. I silently asked God to give me a second chance, then blurted out to Headmaster U Win Kyaing, "Forgive me. I want to come back. Please help me. I ... I can't understand my subjects anymore. And my teachers all hate me now ..."

Smiling, U Win Kyaing reached into my pit of despair — and I took his hand. "I will tutor you every day, Doh Say. But you must be diligent ..."

I had known U Win Kyaing since middle school, and we had often discussed religion and the Bible. Somehow U Win Kyaing mentored me through my final year of high school, and I moved to Taunggyi, the capitol of the Shan State, to attend college.

U Win Kyaing taught me that a Karenni man with character never disrespects God, his parents or his teachers — but I despised my parents and still held most of my teachers in contempt. As for God, he remained to me a Baptist icon — real, but only summoned if I got in trouble.

Light and Run

I rented an apartment in Taunggyi, but before the year was over, I lost interest in my courses at the university.

Without my mentor and friend U Win Kyaing to help me, I struggled with understanding lectures.

I decided to study Chinese kung fu instead ...

Any youth who hiked the jungle trails of the Karenni and Shan States ran the risk of becoming forced labor for the Burma Army or being attacked by wild animals. But in my teens, I carried a religious talisman that I believed made me resistant to harm.

I remembered a story from Sunday school:

A soldier was unconscious for hours before awakening to check a supposed mortal wound. His widowed mother had placed a scripture in his breast pocket before he left home, and where a bullet should have entered his chest, he pulled out a folded-up note with the 23rd Psalm written upon it ...

After hearing the account, I carried a piece of paper in my front pocket, upon which I wrote down the Bible's 23rd Psalm: "The Lord is my shepherd, I lack nothing. He makes me lie down in green pastures, he leads me beside quiet waters, he refreshes my soul. He guides me along the right paths for his name's sake. Even though I walk through the darkest valley, I will fear no evil, for you are with me."

After my academic lapses, I only traveled to Mawchi to ask for money from my parents. At our old house, while my siblings and friends happily bantered in the evening after dinner, I sulked in a corner room like a guilty dog. Everyone ignored me, except Mother.

POWER IN SMILING EYES

She sat beside me on their scuffed bamboo mat and encircled my shoulders with her thin arms. "Doh Say. You're like a stranger to us," she whispered sadly.

Father, stooped and frail, fixed me with sad eyes from across the room, and I threw him a wilting look.

No matter how unkind I acted, my mother and father never refused to help me. They always gave what Kyats (Burmese currency) or food they could spare, which only added to my shame. My heart longed to feel part of my family, but bitterness clouded my good sense.

I traveled back to Loikaw where I took a promising job at my uncle's pharmacy — a trade that should have become my life vocation — but I lasted just a tedious year.

I moved back to Mawchi, familiar stomping grounds. Soon I had no need to ask for money from my parents. I began working at the tin mine making more money than my father had ever dreamed of earning.

࿐࿐࿐

Twist. Strike. Twist. Strike …

I beat memories of shame and failures with a 10-pound sledgehammer. My coworker, U Tin Maung, held an iron drill bit with deft hands as I pounded it 18 inches into solid rock. All day I hand-drilled holes to fill with explosives. We drilled into prospective tungsten and tin veins and set up dynamite charges in layers of rock.

U Tin Maung became a tool in God's hands to convince me to reconcile with my family. Like my teacher,

U Win Kyaing, my mining friend will forever live in my heart.

Light and run.

Like Chinese fireworks, several fuses sizzled at the same time, graduating in length according to the time it took me to escape the explosive salvos.

At 23 years old, I believed that I had discovered my niche. I was known as one of Mawchi's boldest miners, rushing down shafts like a bamboo rat. Hazard pay poured into my pockets like water into a dredge pit — *then out again*, since I squandered most of it away.

After cracking open an ancient hill, dangerous gases sometimes seeped from its bowels. Chemical fumes from the dynamite also lingered inside the treacherous caverns. After a year and a half as a powder monkey, I wondered if I might suffer the same fate as other explosives handlers, whose unmarked graves dotted a hillside nearby.

I lay in my bunk after work, and when I closed my eyes, I relived a near disaster again and again.

My dynamite charge unexpectedly blew rock and debris in range of my crew. Gravel pelted us from the treetops, and one boulder the size of a Tatmadaw jeep careened down the hill to lodge within a few feet of the ditch where we lay. I nervously laughed off the near miss and, after the dust settled, descended the shaft to examine the vein we had ruptured. My lungs pumped like bellows, desperate to filter out chemicals absorbing into my blood.

Now, after sleepless hours in my hammock, the substance still hammered an ache into my brain, and my mind wandered to U Tin Maung's stinging counsel: "I waited 10 years to reconcile with my mother and father. Now I cannot find them. I don't know if they are alive or dead."

U Tin Maung had gazed into the distance as he said, "My foolishness haunts me, Doh Say."

Suddenly, I realized that I was betraying my culture by disrespecting my parents. U Tin Maung convinced me to make peace with my family, and I decided to send money home to help them. It was my duty — but my heart wasn't in it. I applied U Tin Maung's hard lesson to my life, to avoid years of possible misery.

I also weighed the daily hazards I faced as a powder monkey at the Mawchi mine and concluded that it was time to move on.

Tantalizing rumors about men becoming rich overnight enticed me 500 miles north toward China to find the "Stone of Heaven" — Burmese jade — the most sacred and treasured gem in the Far East. One high-grade hunk of jade would buy me respect for a lifetime, and my parents would never have to work again.

I sent a letter home.

"Forgive me for not saying goodbye in person. I am going to dig for jade in the Kachin State. I hope to come home with lots of money ..."

I hiked or purchased seats in passing vehicles as I traveled north toward the legendary jade mines. When I reached Pasaung of Karenni, locals warned me that Burma Army battalions were stopping vehicles, searching for rebels. If soldiers questioned a strong-looking, young buck like me, I might be conscripted as a porter — or worse, a soldier!

I hid for several restless days, often reverently touching my Psalm talisman, and finally I decided not to gamble on my future. The mighty Irrawaddy River flowed nearby, so I found an engineless boat and paddled away — to escape any confrontation with the Tatmadaw.

Curiosity ambushed me as I floated silently past Karenni resistance camps. I wondered if I might see decapitated heads jammed on bamboo poles lining the shore. Grim-looking "rebel" guerrillas pointed and chatted about me, with rifles casually slung over their shoulders.

At school, my government-issue curricula taught me that these men were my sworn enemies, ruthless and bent upon destroying Burma. But none of the rebels raised a rifle barrel in my direction.

I decided to land and speak to them.

They called themselves freedom fighters with the Karenni National Progressive Party (KNPP), and they wore a hodge-podge of castoff, tattered camouflage uniforms, bandanas and bush hats. Though war-hardened and gaunt, they laughed and talked with me like we sat in a noodle shop in Loikaw.

Most soldiers carried AK-47s or M-16s, and I dearly wished to shoot one of the military weapons. I had no intention of joining their cause, because the green Stone of Heaven still commandeered my dreams.

POWER IN SMILING EYES

Several miles from the jade mines, I dragged the leaky teak dugout onto a bank to share rice with a large contingent of resistance fighters. Our conversation drifted toward my hometown of Mawchi, and one soldier remarked, "I know your cousin, Erreh. He's at our camp headquarters right now!"

Finding a family member — and a rebel! — in such a remote place fascinated me. I glanced at my boat, then at the barefoot warriors squatting around the campfire.

Do these men get up every morning with purpose in their hearts? What possesses a man to risk his life fighting the Burma Army? Maybe cousin Erreh can tell me.

At first light, I followed the soldiers through the tangle of forest and arrived at the Karenni headquarters, winded but proud that I kept their pace.

A soldier who knew Erreh told me, "He's on the frontlines. I'm on the way to the fighting in the morning. You wanna come?"

I longingly eyed his M-16, nodding. "And maybe I can shoot your rifle?"

He laughed and said, "I'll get you a gun to carry — and a pack."

We bedded down for the night, and the next morning we began our two-day "marathon march" up and down mountains in 100-plus-degree heat. I was dead on my feet and wanted to drop my heavy M-16 off a cliff. At one of our few rest breaks, the soldier let me shoot two rounds.

Cousin Erreh was a captain and chief medic with the KNPP and had little time to reminisce about family. His arms and hands were red with dried blood, and men were limping or being dragged into his tent.

A steep gorge separated the Karenni fighters and the Tatmadaw. Rag-tag Karenni troops moved like panthers — from tree to trench to rocks for cover — firing until they ran out of ammo.

The fog of war overwhelmed me. For days, I had shared the food and fires with Karenni brothers, listening to eyewitnesses speak of Tatmadaw bloodshed and destruction in their villages.

"They kill our families and steal our land," they told me. "*That's* why we fight!"

I was beginning to understand the fear in my father's eyes when he passed Burma soldiers back home. And, for the first time, I *believed* the students at my college in Taunggyi, who whispered about the torture and murders of suspected "rebel collaborators."

Freedom fighters came to Medic Erreh, limbless and screaming, while other resistance soldiers rushed to occupy their places. My inner tally of atrocities suddenly reached a flashpoint, and I grabbed my borrowed M-16 to join a group of soldiers running to the firing line.

The fantasy of uncovering a hunk of choicest jade lost every bit of its luster that day.

Mortar fire and machine-gun spatter died out, like a gradual clearing after a thunderstorm. Karenni soldiers regrouped away from the front, and I assisted my cousin as he tended to more wounded men.

POWER IN SMILING EYES

Suddenly, Erreh stood up and saluted in the direction of the tent doorway. A very thin officer in fatigues entered with two armed guards. General Aung Than Lay, commander of the Karenni Army, spoke encouragingly to the wounded men on blankets and shook my cousin's hand.

"Good work, Captain."

When the general nodded to me, I felt naked. I was the only man in the tent who wasn't a Karenni freedom fighter, but the general memorized my face that day. I remained a volunteer soldier at my cousin's camp for weeks, helping dig trenches and graves and carrying supplies.

One day, I received a dispatch from General Aung Than Lay. He wished to see me.

In a primitive bamboo field shelter, I stood in the presence of a man who had been fighting for Karenni independence since World War II. The general seemed to have knowledge of who I was.

"You are a hard worker, Doh Say. And you speak English. Can you read and write?"

"Yes, sir. And I want to join the resistance."

The future Karenni prime minister smiled at me, then faced a map on the wall thoughtfully. He had made his decision.

"There are many ways to fight our enemy, Doh Say. We need a man like you to work with our allies at the KNU (Karen National Union) headquarters at Manerplaw, near the Thai border. I had my first diplomacy training there. You will study to become an officer, too."

My general patiently heard me out as I explained that I was better suited for frontlines action than desk work — but he wouldn't budge.

"You can serve your Karenni people best by using your skills at Manerplaw."

How could I disobey an order from such a great man? I opened my heart to my commander — though grubbing for jade really seemed more appealing than learning to be a military bureaucrat.

But I never arrived at Manerplaw.

I waited impatiently for weeks near one of the KNPP training headquarters, helping medics. The Burma Army dealt a decisive blow against the resistance in the Manerplaw region, and the battle for Htar Na Kwe rescued me from what I considered a boring future.

I blended into the rank and file guerrilla infantry for nearly a year, a volunteer fighter in the Karenni Army. I marched as a vigilante soldier and studied armaments and tactics from military books loaned to me. I received my training with AK-47s, RPGs and other weapons from friends on the field of battle.

"A Blind Man is Never Afraid of Ghosts"
(Ancient Burmese saying)

I had intimate knowledge of explosives from my work at the Mawchi tin mine. The essence of dynamite still ran in my blood, but I had never *felt* a direct blast or seen the effect of shrapnel on the human body. Setting charges was far different than lying in a trench while 120mm mortars exploded around me. The Tatmadaw launched explosives at us by the hundreds, designed to concuss and stun or slice us to pieces with bits of shell casings. Mortars left deep gouges in the earth that we used as foxholes.

It was a confusing, sad afternoon during which a few friends had taken direct hits. I followed a couple of soldiers at a dead run toward a great hardwood tree the size of a jet's fuselage. In minutes, the Burma Army honed in on our position, and the tree exploded, its massive limbs crashing to the earth around us.

We lay in the bottom of a mortar trench, and a bomb sighed above our heads before dropping in our hideout. We scattered away from the projectile like termites in a spotlight, waiting for its tapered shell to detonate, but nothing happened. As I crawled away from the sizzling dud, I reached into my shirt and fingered my folded-up 23rd Psalm on scraps of paper — one in each breast pocket.

I had doubled my luck by placing an identical chapter of Psalm 23 in my other pocket. I seldom thought about God, but I did today. I thought God had saved me again because I carried my talismans! Mistakenly, I believed that I was favored among these men wounded by Burma Army bullets and shrapnel.

ॐॐॐ

About three hours from the Thai-Burma border, in the Southern Karenni State, the Tatmadaw launched a fresh offensive, and our forces valiantly held the line for four days. The enemy's tactics never changed: shelling first to soften us up, then overwhelming us with a full battalion armed to the teeth.

On this fateful day, Erreh sustained wounds, and I seethed with anger as I followed my commander into a furious engagement. Our RPGs had been effective, and we advanced on the Burma Army's positions, tripping over bodies and firing our rifles as we kept the pressure up. I'm not sure that I hit a single enemy soldier, but I fired in their general direction.

Suddenly a tinny-sounding whistle rang out, and I knew it signaled that a Tatmadaw battalion would soon mount a steady, relentless ground attack. We would be "scythed" like rice stalks when they gained the field. It was time to run for cover into the mountains.

On a steep, rocky hill, I felt the first bullet enter my back. Before I hit the ground, two other rounds from an automatic weapon pierced my torso and spun lead against my innards. One of the bullets tore into my lung. Another lost momentum and lodged in my belly. I rolled downhill like a sack of rice thrown from a truck and finally slid into a pile of sharp boulders.

I held tight to consciousness, taking deep, painful breaths, and dragged myself away from where I surmised the Burma Army advanced. Between blackouts, I spoke with God, *very* confused.

POWER IN SMILING EYES

I trust you so much that my two pockets are full of your lucky Bible verses — why didn't you save me this time?

It was one of the few moments since childhood that I earnestly spoke to God — it was reasonable, since I might be meeting him face to face.

And God spoke to my heart: *Doh Say, it's time to change your direction.* I felt weak, but I stubbornly resisted God's urging. He said, *Know me, Doh Say! And forgive your parents. Let me change your heart.*

"No! I cannot."

But look at your wounds! And look where you might end up!

In my mind, I suddenly saw hell, while blood gushed from my wounds like water from ruptured pipes.

Oh, very terrible! I cannot take this. I cannot die now!

I prayed in an unconscious yet very *real* state of mind: "Jesus. Okay, okay ... I give up. My life is yours. And I will love my parents. I promise."

I lay on my side, very still, while an image of Jesus and the faces of my mother and father drifted across my consciousness. I groaned aloud, marking a final plunge into darkness. I opened my eyes one last time while two figures leaned over me. The last sounds I heard were *friendly* voices. And sadly, I later learned, the bullets that struck me were from friendly fire.

My nightfall lasted for five days, and when I regained consciousness, I felt like my future had been blasted to pieces.

꙲꙲꙲

I convalesced in a camp with thousands of bamboo huts and 5,000 other refugees. Helpless as an infant, I lay in my cot all day and night, looking forward to a ration of rice twice a day. Waiting for my wounds to heal felt like watching bananas ripen on a tree — mind-numbingly slow.

For months, the nerve endings around my infected bullet wounds screamed at the slightest touch of clothing. I retreated into a skeletal shadow of my former robust self, and when attendants helped me stand, I moved like a grotesquely bent cripple.

I'm 27 and look like a 90-year-old hunchback. But I am alive!

The 23rd Psalm lived in my heart now, and not in my shirt pockets:

"Yea, though I walk through the valley of the shadow of death, I will fear no evil, for thou art with me ..."

Jesus had saved my life and bridled my reckless spirit. I was fully dependent upon him to help me survive each day. Attendants fed me. Nurses cleaned my wounds. I lived in a room with dozens of other bedridden men, my self-centered, solitary life stripped away like dirty bandages. God had complete control of my future and enrolled me in the school of patience.

Though I was skin and bones physically, my soul grew healthy, and my faith ran steep mountains every day. Cured of bitterness, God's love replaced a seething discontent in my heart. The staff at the refugee camp channeled God's mercy into my life.

I had much time to reflect upon my family in Mawchi. My parents had passed away, and I wished I could have been at their bedsides when they died.

While my body healed in a safe place away from the battlefield, God provided rigorous training for my mind. Each morning and evening for nearly two years, I studied with a Christian evangelist who taught me lessons from God's word through a radio broadcast. Wherever attendants moved me, making room for new casualties, my radio teacher followed me.

When I grew strong enough, I hobbled to church services held every Sunday, where pastors from several denominations took turns preaching to our transient congregation. Adversity made us ethnics one in heart. We were survivors scarred by evil but determined to return to our homeland and take up the fight for freedom again.

But how do you fight, Doh Say, now that you are a cripple?

I could never power through a forced march again. How could I carry a rifle or stack heavy boxes of ammo on the frontlines?

ৡৡৡ

Statesman Aung Than Lay — former POW; former Commander-in-Chief, Karenni Army; Chairman, Karenni National Progressive Party; and now, Karenni Prime

Minister — visited injured troops at our refugee camp.

And he recognized *me*.

I struggled to snap to attention, but only my salute was crisp and strong. The prime minister lived at a temporary home at the edge of the refugee camp when he wasn't trying to spearhead unity meetings or fortifying military ties among Burma's ethnic groups.

"Doh Say? Come to my house; we should talk," he said warmly.

Well-armed Karenni resistance fighters stood guard at our refugee camp and especially around Aung Than Lay's home.

He welcomed me as a fellow Karenni warrior, and in his stern but gentle way, reminded me of his desire for me to receive officer training. "I think you should enter diplomatic service for our people. Your English is good."

Politics fascinated me, and I limped to the prime minister's home often to pore over history books he loaned me. When I grew stronger, I became his steward, and while I served his important guests drinks or plates of fruit, I listened and learned from a Karenni master diplomat.

The prime minister was a gifted listener to smooth politicians and angry ethnic leaders and also to distraught Karenni soldiers and foreign diplomats. After an audience with Aung Than Lay, his guests left the conference room satisfied, feeling like they had finished a fine meal.

I seized this unique opportunity to learn the art of mediation, and the prime minister sent me to the Karen

State for intense training in international law and diplomacy.

I had buried the self-absorbed, angry Doh Say on a bloody Burma mountain. The reborn Doh Say discovered fulfillment working as an official with the Karenni Foreign Ministry. I filled the post for nearly a decade, ending my career as the Karenni Director of Foreign Ministry.

And whenever I traveled to the refugee camp, the prime minister, my friend, left his door open for me to stay at his home.

**"This is not a revolutionary war. It is a resistance war.
They [the Burma Army] are invaders."**
— *Aung Than Lay, Karenni Prime Minister*

In 1997, our Karenni foreign affairs office buzzed with news about a first-ever conference organized by a well-respected American missionary. More than 100 delegates from states and divisions all over Burma were invited to the Ethnic Nationalities Seminar at Mae Tha Ra Hta, in Eastern Karen State. The conference convened for two electrifying weeks, and this Christian ex-Special Forces soldier opened each meeting with a moment of silent prayer.

The American — as fluent in the Thai language as a native — obviously understood the diversity of cultures represented at the conference, and he tirelessly coordinated peaceful discussions between ethnic leaders who had been bitter enemies.

This Christian missionary, Dave Eubank, made no apologies for his demonstrative faith in God, and he ardently opposed the scorched-earth policy of the Tatmadaw, aimed at innocent villagers in Burma.

After the meeting at Mae Tha Ra Hta, back at my Karenni Foreign Ministry office, I described the unprecedented spirit of cooperation that I observed. Ethnic leaders had adjourned with a new sense of anticipation and looked forward to another conference the following year.

Gathering the delegates from the jungle villages, mountain hamlets, guerilla hideouts and cities was nothing short of miraculous, and Eubank, a former U.S. Army major, boldly touted Jesus as the power behind the achievement.

For the first time in war-ravaged Burma, ethnic heads of state from different regions had composed a document outlining their vision for a unified and *free* Burma.

I decided that Dave Eubank was a man I needed to know for political reasons.

ૐૐૐ

During the years between 1997 and 2001, while I served as a member of the Karenni Foreign Ministry, the reorganized central government of Burma (State Peace and Development Council) expanded its deadly reach into the frontier areas of Burma.

The same year that we ethnics adjourned the Mae Tha

POWER IN SMILING EYES

Ra Hta conference with optimism in 1997, the Burma Army unleashed the bloodiest offensives in history against the Karen, Karenni and Shan States. Internally displaced people fled to the mountains and jungles by the thousands.

Ill-equipped resistance forces "pushed back," but in almost every faceoff between the guerrillas and the Burma Army, the freedom fighters lost.

During these desperate years, a cadre of resistance-fighters-turned-relief-workers marched to the frontlines to rescue, feed and medically treat the villagers living at or near hide sites in the Burma jungles. These mostly ethnic nationals called themselves the Free Burma Rangers and were led by the missionary Dave Eubank.

Recognizing the desperation of their people, the Karen, Karenni and Shan leaders in the resistance movement supported the Free Burma Rangers whenever they marched into their districts.

They supplied reconnaissance, communications and armed scouts and encouraged men and women in their own ranks to train with Dave Eubank at his training camps.

The numbers of IDPs receiving relief and medical treatment grew from hundreds to thousands.

A few months after the Mae Tha Ra Hta conference, I became involved in a frenzy of diplomatic work near my old refugee camp. Dave Eubank worked nearby, at the Free Burma Rangers headquarters, and we often traveled on the same roads.

I had gained back strength and stamina that surpassed my endurance even as a young tin miner and soldier, and I recognized my physical recovery as a gift from Jesus. I had no idea that my endurance would be key in my work with the Free Burma Rangers someday.

Dave and I jounced along many rutted miles together and shared our life stories. Over the years, I felt a peculiar bond forming between us, but I kept tripping over one of his idiosyncrasies that shaped all his relationships and decisions.

"Let's pray right now, Doh Say. Okay?"

In the truck. At a restaurant. Among government officials. Or with the prime minister himself! Dave didn't hesitate. He prayed with anyone, for anyone, *anywhere.*

It embarrassed me at first. But I grew to appreciate his spontaneous acknowledgment that he needed God *right now* to be present and active. God's peace covered us each time he called on Jesus for help, and I began to pray more often, too.

In 1998, Dave officially requested permission from our Karenni government to travel by foot with a caravan bearing relief supplies to IDPs living just outside a "black zone." As usual, the Tatmadaw had scattered deadly landmines around vacated Karenni villages to keep our people from returning to collect belongings and food stores.

Any Karenni discovered hiding in the black zone was "eliminated" or relocated to special camps from which the Tatmadaw officers conscripted laborers. And Burma

POWER IN SMILING EYES

Army snipers acted upon orders to kill anyone setting foot in this black zone.

"Dave, you might be captured or shot. Or you might fall prey to the *invisible* enemy."

I meant landmines.

"I know you were a Special Forces soldier, and maybe you could fight your way through, but you cannot fight what you cannot *see*!"

A scar "crater" in my back twinged, and I remembered wounds that took years to heal. I had carried my share of landmine victims off the frontlines many times.

"Doh Say, look at me, friend."

Dave sat silent for a few seconds, then he said, "We are all God's children. I need to go. And if I lose my legs, it's up to God. If I *die*, it's up to God."

I reluctantly helped Dave gain approval for a relief mission in the Karenni State and joined his family in praying for his safe return. He and his Rangers completed the mission and came home after many weeks of dodging the Tatmadaw.

Dave's pioneer journey through our Karenni jungle broke ground for relief workers to return with caravans of food and supplies for thousands of desperate IDPs in the following years.

అఇఅఇఅఇ

I had joined our decades-old resistance war to defeat the "invaders" in my Karenni homeland. My goals included stoking international outrage by reporting the SPDC's agenda.

I helped apply diplomatic "barbs" to guide the Burma government into negotiations with us. I believed that, over time, we politicians could persuade the Burma junta to allow free elections and support changes to implement a democratic form of governing the nation.

But in the years I worked at the Foreign Ministry, we at the KNPP and our guerrilla counterparts couldn't stem the tide of well-armed and technologically advanced Tatmadaw offensives. I had failed to hit my intended target.

As a well-respected diplomat at the Foreign Ministry, I had great political ambitions. But one day, while carrying a rucksack full of medical supplies to IDPs with the Free Burma Rangers, I stood upon another mountain of decision.

From 2001 through 2004, I had read hundreds of field reports documenting the plight of the internally displaced people, but my face-to-face encounters with these plundered souls now cut me to the quick.

I identified with their helpless rage. I heard their wails of utter hopelessness. I sensed the fathomless grief of a father holding the burned remains of his children. Muddy, diseased orphans clung to one another, and long lines of IDPs ignored the agonies of hiking with bloody bare feet. A mother stumbled on a trail with a toddler in each arm and two other children tied to her back and chest. Fevered men rested in cold rain puddles with un-bandaged open wounds. Few IDPs had blankets. Most foraged in the jungle for food.

Homeless and helpless, if the IDPs heard sporadic, distant gunfire, they cringed, ready to run — but which way? Their eyes begged me for help, and my fulfillment as a soldier, a diplomat and an aspiring politician felt *used up.*

No armed or political resistance could staunch this invasion of evil coursing through the world's veins. God had spared my life and healed my body, and now he reignited a restlessness in my heart that I hadn't felt since I was a young man. I sensed a new mission, but balked at my ability to take the challenge.

Pray for your enemies, Doh Say.

I can't, God! Not the Tatmadaw.

But I tried, and the words finally tumbled out. "Okay, Jesus. Change the hearts of my enemy. Cause them to retreat and leave the villagers alone so that our people can live in their homes again. And save the soldiers in the Burma Army from this evil, too."

On this mountain of decision, I enrolled in training to be a servant leader. Every mission I seized thereafter, I acknowledged as belonging to God. In fact, my heavy burden of saving our nation from invaders suddenly belonged to Jesus, and *not me.*

When I left my post as a Karenni diplomat, I felt as free as when I set that last charge at the Mawchi tin mine! Dave Eubank asked me to help him train Free Burma Rangers, and my ambition hit a bedrock of fulfillment.

Deep in the jungles of the Karen State, Shan State and among my beloved Karenni people, I am a diplomat for Jesus. A man who seldom measures time as he listens to displaced people whose humanity is violated and hope ruined. Hours pass. They tell me their stories — crucial knowledge for the next generation living in Burma who, God willing, can change our nation.

Blessed Ridgeline

I am wounded in heart when I think of my brothers and sisters who live in Mawchi, because the Burma Army controls their lives now. It's been 23 years since I have been home, and I grieve, knowing what my loved ones must be suffering.

But to ease my sorrow, God has added family to my life wherever I travel.

Good Life Club children call out, "Uncle Doh Say!" and when one looks into my smiling eyes, God speaks comfort to us both.

Helping direct the Good Life Club with other Free Burma Rangers came as naturally to me as singing. We carry our GLC program to as few as two or three shivering children and to as many as 500 kids flocking from villages and hide sites.

Mothers live in constant fear for their children, whose bare feet may touch off landmines where they play. We admire and love these brave women and do our best to lift their spirits and meet their needs, too.

POWER IN SMILING EYES

Women and children are the most vulnerable members of the displaced people in Burma, and Dave's wife, Karen, has succeeded in adding the Good Life Club program to every FBR relief mission in Burma. Our program can be rolled out in minutes now (sometimes between mortar shellings), and we tailor every GLC to the culture where the families live.

I am a GLC member whose work through the years has included: setting safe itineraries, translating languages, babysitting, changing diapers, cooking, digging latrines and garbage holes, delivering babies, treating wounds, praying for sick children, tending pack ponies and physically protecting my innocent charges — *especially Karen Eubank and her children.*

During our GLCs, we Rangers tell Bible stories through drama, feed the children snacks, give health lessons and play games. Singing is our centerpiece, and our talented musicians strum guitars to accompany songs.

Free Burma Rangers medics set up clinics to treat anyone who is ill, and at the end of the GLC program, we happily unload our heavy packs and distribute clothing, mosquito nets and school supplies to needy parents. Supporters around the world send gifts to "kit out" the Good Life Club so we can supply dedicated teachers school books and financial help.

The shyest children and most guarded parents cannot resist laughing with us grown men as we dance and cavort to songs we teach the children. When it's time to pack up and move to another hide site or village, they beg us to stay. They ask us to sing the same songs over and over because we are no longer strangers, but *family*.

છે–છે–છે

On a barren hill, a Tatmadaw battalion pinned down a handful of us Rangers as we guarded the slow retreat of about 400 grandparents, fathers, mothers and children. In this rugged area of the Karen State, the Burma Army had been burning homes and terrorizing anyone who had been captured.

Dave's wife and kids were conducting a Good Life Club program at a village guarded by Karen soldiers, about two hours away. Dave hadn't seen his family for nearly 10 days. After praying, he felt assured that his loved ones were in good hands with the Karen people, if the Tatmadaw mobilized in their direction.

We had just returned to this barren knoll after fulfilling a promise to deliver medicine to sick and dying IDPs at a hide site nearly 50 miles away. Our FBR team wearily stood guard as IDPs evacuated a village below us — but bullets have a way of reloading adrenaline, no matter how tired a Ranger feels.

From our vantage, we watched a KNLA security man pull the trigger of his M-16 as he aimed at approaching enemy soldiers — but nothing happened. A second soldier leveled his old flintlock, but his weapon misfired. Our third security man launched an M-79 grenade in the enemy's general direction — and then all three lit out!

POWER IN SMILING EYES

Along the bottom of our barren hill, the three KNLA soldiers skittered like nimble monkeys, keeping a few paces ahead of machine-gun spray. They had missed or misread radio chatter and mistakenly thought that the enemy battalion was still an hour away from our position.

Our previous 10 days had been packed with turmoil and God's gracious help. Five thousand IDPs stumbled along trails in small disorganized groups all over the Northern Karen State. We were helping everyone that we could.

Eliya Samson had delivered one healthy baby boy inside a bamboo lean-to. His mother wanted us to name him, so Dave named him Alexander Solzhenitsyn.

A rice grower had been captured by the Tatmadaw and tortured before he escaped, but his farm had been laced with landmines. The invisible enemy exploded beneath a teenager's sandal, carving the flesh from one leg. Our chief medic, Eliya, had clamped his femoral artery before he bled out, and I joined a pole-sling relay team, bearing the boy partway to a medical facility.

Mortars were landing helter-skelter in nearly every direction we traveled.

The barren mountaintop where we dug in was quickly turning to a moonscape from incoming 60mm mortar rounds, rocket-propelled grenades, rifle grenades and machine-gun bullets. From my experience on the field of battle, I knew each ballistic tremor by heart, and I prayed that Dave and our team was safe.

I had one 30-round clip that I was saving. Our team

had agreed not to fire at the Burma Army soldiers unless the battalion was certain to overrun our position to attack the IDPs.

My eyes were riveted upon a rice field between the enemy and us, waiting for the soul-freezing Tatmadaw tin whistle, signaling their all-out charge. I prayed that the officer would decide not to send his troops forward. It was sure to be bloody and likely the last time we particular Rangers ever helped IDPs.

I rooted my mind behind my bullet-scarred tree while the deafening barrage continued. I lay still, my AK-47 silent but aimed toward more soldiers than I could ever hope to intercept.

"Doh Say! We're pulling back! Doh Say!"

Dave was screaming, but his voice blended with the barrage. My ears rang like a dynamite charge had just exploded somewhere near, and suddenly I felt a hand on my shoulder. Dave crouched beside me.

"Didn't you hear me? It's time to go, Brother!"

I hesitated, looking back at the brow of the hill. "I'll leave when everybody is safe."

Dave sat on his haunches with me, a perfect, big Caucasian target.

"We're all safe! The IDPs, too! Doh Say! Come on!"

Dave had dashed 50 yards across open ground in broad daylight to save me, and now he was about to run it again! I grasped his arm. "Lord Jesus?" I prayed over the scream of a mortar, "Protect us!"

And we ran.

POWER IN SMILING EYES

Our boots barely grazed the top of our barren hill. We dived below the blessed ridgeline, then down an embankment to join our retreating comrades. Our 400 IDPs were nowhere in sight and far out of mortar range.

Warrior Uncle

I am in charge of all FBR missions in the Karenni State now, and I help coordinate the Good Life Club program for the Free Burma Rangers, too. But it's my work as God's courier where my faith is tested most often. I sometimes feel like I'm running that 50-yard dash again, a target for the enemy.

On my solitary missions into the Karenni jungle, I pack very light. I must focus on the trail at least 100 feet ahead of me to keep from surprising a wild boar or Tatmadaw soldiers. It's best to see them first.

I sleep like a wary panther. I sling my hammock low, near the jungle floor to keep my body below the line of small-arms fire and to stay where exploding mortars are less likely to fling shrapnel. I sleep far from roads and trails, concealed from human eyes.

At 46 years old, I purposely live in the same conditions as my 160 Karenni schoolteachers to whom I deliver modest salaries for their teaching supplies and work. Many have taught students at hide sites for years for no pay at all, but through generous gifts from an organization called Partners Relief and Development, the Free Burma Rangers now supports their selfless efforts.

They teach about the true history of our Karenni State and about our ongoing struggle to recover our national sovereignty.

"Who guards all that money you carry, Doh Say?" Karenni leaders ask me sometimes. "How many soldiers come with you?"

"Two of us," I tell them. "Me and ..." I point to heaven.

At times I have traveled so close to the Burma Army patrols that I could hear them whisper, but God blinded their eyes. For years, I have refused a security detail, except to be led through landmine areas by local guides.

For protection, I depend upon the powerful prayers of my FBR team and the loving intercessions by people around the world who know my name.

And I rely upon the prayers of children who love Doh Say, their uncle with smiling eyes.

CHAPTER 6
LENS OF THE SHEPHERD
KA PAW SAY'S STORY

"If we die, who will take care of our families?
God is taking care of us (Rangers), and he will
take care of our families, too."
Ka Paw Say — Team Pastor,
Chief Videographer, Free Burma Rangers

Truth in the Crosshairs

Families who live in Burma tread carefully into the 21st century, like we cross a rotting bamboo bridge. The world calls this bridge democracy. We ethnics hold our collective breath, praying it will hold us up, while deception and treachery roil beneath us.

I was a Karenni soldier, trained for combat. I lived and breathed to fight, yet I never lined up crosshairs on a single Tatmadaw soldier until I joined the Free Burma Rangers. Now I focus camera optics on Burma Army patrols and "shoot" soldiers while they clear acres of stolen land to build roads, airstrips, helipads, barracks and wardrooms. I record displaced villagers suffering from campaigns of ethnic cleansing.

RANGERS IN THE GAP

Diplomats insist that attacks on civilians by the Burma Army don't happen anymore. But wounded villagers tell my camera a different story. I unearth heart-wrenching accounts from fathers and mothers tortured by rogue Tatmadaw officers. I run ahead of the FBR pack trains with Karenni guerrillas to film burning homes and panicked IDPs who feel the bridge of democracy collapsing under their sandals.

ๆๆๆ

Free Burma Rangers often work in the shadow of death, but humor blunts the sharp burrs on our care-worn nerves. We name our team leaders after personality traits or defining events: We call Eliya Samson, our chief medic, Mad Dog; Doh Say, our Karenni State team coordinator, Vulture; and Saw Sun, our Karen State team coordinator, Koala Bear.

My friends call me Monkey. It's an affectionate nickname fished from a growing pool of talented soldiers, medics, schoolteachers, preachers, students, secretaries, mechanics, doctors, nurses, CEOs, engineers and others who work as part of our international team.

Fifteen years ago, I traded my M-16 for a video camera, but there are times that the Burma Army has forced me to grab a rifle again to defend my comrades or villagers from slaughter. And some days, no matter how much you plan and pray, uncertainty steals your high ground.

LENS OF THE SHEPHERD

Our KNLA (Karen National Liberation Army) radioman had intercepted chatter about a Tatmadaw battalion marching toward a cluster of villages where Dave Eubank's wife, son and daughters and FBR team members medically treated and encouraged IDPs.

I packed my camera safely in my rucksack as soon as Dave began briefing us.

"We have one day to position ourselves between the Burma Army and the villagers evacuating their homes in the valley below us. We must delay the Tatmadaw here, to give villagers a chance to escape."

"Don't you want to leave us and find your family?" a soldier asked Dave.

He shook his head. "Karen and the kids know how to fall back in a hurry. And they are with good Rangers who will help them." He said it with finality. "We've radioed the villagers to get out."

I glanced at Eliya Samson and Doh Say. With only 21 Karen resistance fighters, we were no match for the well-armed soldiers a few miles away. We had little ammunition, and our brave Karen security team shouldered WWII and other vintage rifles. We double-timed to a ravine where Dave split us into three groups to appear more numerous and formidable than we were.

We Rangers gathered for prayer as our Karen fighters nervously dug in. Immediately the assault began, as always, *in our minds.*

"Lord Jesus, are we doing the right thing? What if the Burma Army doesn't take a defensive position like they usually do? How can we share the love of Christ with soldiers we may shoot at?"

Dusk had turned pitch-black. None of us wanted to be martyrs, but for the sake of the defenseless, fleeing villagers, we resolved not to let the Tatmadaw move past us this night.

Cooking pots clanked in rucksacks from the ravine, and Dave turned to me. "Monkey, we may be killing people tonight. Is this what God wants?"

I took a deep breath. "We have prayed, and I believe that God has given us his answer. *This* is God's place for us," I whispered. "Anyway, most of our guns don't even work!"

Our angst vanished in the thickening darkness as we chuckled together. Our guerrilla comrades must have thought we were losing our minds.

We could see the lantern lights below us and hear the mounting clatter of a military column. We knew from previous reports that we sat above 400 Burma Army soldiers snaking through the ravine. In a village we had just visited, an officer had ordered a man beheaded — his unit had displayed the bloody skull on a bamboo stake. Several men and women had been shot as they ran to hide in the jungle.

Dave and I prayed as we listened, knowing our tactical window of engagement was closing.

"Lord God. Let none of us on this hill be harmed. Keep the villagers safe. And cause the Burma Army to retreat! Keep every one of them safe, too!"

LENS OF THE SHEPHERD

It was an *illogical* prayer: We were outraged and wanted to retaliate. Witnessing Tatmadaw brutality was bitter and fresh in our minds.

It was an *impossible* prayer: KNLA soldiers usually booby-trapped sections of path that the Burma Army traveled. Tatmadaw point men would certainly trip an explosion. And, in a 400-man battalion, *some* soldiers would die from hit-and-run guerrilla ambushes.

Then, without warning, as suddenly as it began, the clanking in the ravine melted away.

"Do you hear them anymore, Ka Paw Say?" Dave whispered to me.

I listened, *hard.*

"Not anymore."

Four hundred Tatmadaw troops had disappeared.

Our motley crew of Rangers and Karen guerrillas never drew down upon a single Burma Army soldier. Nor could other groups of Karen fighters find this dreaded battalion to ambush them as they marched away. They became noises in the night, targets for our prayers alone. We stayed for hours in our positions, straining to hear.

We'll never have a rational explanation for why the enemy turned back minutes before we engaged them. In the heat of our crisis, we had accepted God's *peace* as his answer, and we prayerfully acted upon it. God spared our lives, the villagers *and* the lives of our enemy.

ᄽᄽᄽ

My brave, persevering grandfather shepherded congregations in several communities in the Karenni State. He was a pastor during the turbulent '70s and '80s, when the Burma government first zeroed in on regions suspected of supporting resistance fighters. To sever any pipelines for supplying food to the so-called rebels, the Burma Army ordered villages vacated.

Forcing families to hastily rebuild shacks after burning their ancestral farms triggered emotional convulsions that shattered the Karenni and Karen cultures. Burma Army officers platted the controlled areas where villagers could legally relocate, but some people were too elderly or poor to start over. They traveled to villages where relatives took them in.

The Burma Army confiscated or butchered the farmers' livestock, and the merciless jungle overran productive rice fields that villagers had cultivated for generations.

With this cruel military strategy, the government would ultimately control the border regions of the Karen and Karenni States.

My apostolic grandfather founded houses of worship wherever villagers were forced to resettle and hiked a circuit to visit each church as their traveling pastor.

When Grandfather spent time in our village, he stayed at our small bamboo house with my father, mother and eight of my siblings.

My parents were active in our Baptist church and taught me Bible principles that they hoped I might live by.

LENS OF THE SHEPHERD

Father was a praying man, and his lifestyle stamped an image upon my conscience that I have never forgotten.

When I was a boy, my family moved to Loikaw, Karenni State, where Father found work. I walked to my government school every day, and for some years, I planned to become an engineer. I excelled in my studies due to a gift of dogged concentration and problem solving.

But the year of my graduation, a distraction gained power over me. In 10th grade, I fell head over heels in love with a young woman who was four years older than me.

Shame.

I failed my final exams, and my college ambitions vanished, along with the romance. At home, I couldn't raise my head to look my father in the eye. I abandoned my family to live with relatives who needed help at their rice mill.

The people in my new Karenni hometown mixed with the Burma Army like curry and rice. Amiable soldiers walked our streets, evoking respect and reinforcing what I had always been taught in the government school. They were our protectors, to be obeyed and esteemed. It was the Karenni rebels who must be feared. Burma citizens were instructed to hand over information about subversives, which would have been easy. The barracks and training grounds for the Burma Army lay within shouting distance of where I lived with my cousin.

At about 3 a.m., I sat a few paces from my cousin's house, *thinking*. I missed my family, but I *was* happy. I had Kyats coming in from my work operating a rice-hulling machine at the mill, and I planned to advance in my uncle's business over time.

I was nearly finished with my present business in the outhouse when I heard the first mortars sing and explode from the direction of the Burma Army camp. Several others followed, and I yawned.

Must be gunnery practice again.

I wondered what it was like to fire a rifle or machine gun like the ones I heard firing now. Suddenly, my cousin's voice rose above the shelling. "Ka Paw Say! Come out of there, you idiot! There's a battle going on!"

I burst from the outhouse, but my cousin was only a voice in the dawn. Flashes lit up the sky, and my heart beat like a Karenni drum. I heard mumblings from my cousin's house, and I bounded inside just in time to see the door to a basement hideout slam shut. My relatives had dug a bulletproof room under a portion of my cousin's house, just in case the Karenni resistance and the Tatmadaw ever clashed outside.

But neighbors borrowed all the space in my cousin's bunker and weren't about to share a pin-feather's inch. Hoarse rebukes stopped me from crawling into what looked like too many geese in a cage.

Bullets ripped through the thin bamboo walls of my cousin's living room, and I leaped outside to belly under another part of the house. Round after round ricocheted off a stack of wood that I curled up behind. Hours passed, and the firefight died down to sporadic gunfire. Soldiers began patrolling the street.

LENS OF THE SHEPHERD

Karenni guerrillas!

They ordered my panicked neighbors and relatives out of their hideout and motioned me from my crawlspace, too.

"You need to leave," an officer said quietly. "Come."

About a dozen of us crouched in a gulley outside of our village, listening. Close combat raged for a while, but suddenly the shooting died to sporadic rifle bursts as all souls in uniform were finished off.

Who had won?

We villagers emerged from hiding, quietly. The Karenni resistance had enjoyed a short-lived victory, but now the Tatmadaw dragged their dead soldiers into piles. Suddenly, the shock of seeing dozens of charred homes seized us.

Only blackened upright posts stood intact where my uncle and aunt had raised their children. I watched my broken uncle shuffle toward his rice mill — his family's livelihood for a generation. Hulling equipment had twisted from intense heat inside his bamboo barns. Tons of rice and thousands of Kyats in business capital blended with the ashes.

I didn't care who burned my uncle out. I just knew that I had nowhere to go. My grandfather would have told me, "Pray for your enemies, Ka Paw Say. Forgive them."

So, I fashioned a prayer: "God, these Karenni guerrillas are so evil. Show them the light."

When my mother heard about the tragedy, she sent my brother to fetch me home.

Uprising

My family could barely afford it, but they sent me to technical school at Loikaw where I ranked highly in my chosen pursuits: drinking, smoking, chewing betel nut, carousing. I spent two years "studying" engineering and stumbling down the path of failure.

The bloody 8888 Uprising saved me from total academic humiliation. Thousands of students, Buddhist monks and civilians gathered in the streets of the capitals in Burma to protest the repressive junta and demand a democratically elected prime minister and parliament.

I couldn't have cared less about the history-making democracy movement. I stayed at home, happy that the doors to our college were chained shut. The streets of Loikaw swelled with student protesters, many whom I knew. Then, as if the order came from hell itself, the Tatmadaw began to imprison students to quell their demonstrations.

Students abandoned homes and college forever and gathered in small groups to join Karenni resistance fighters in the mountains. Almost all my school chums joined the KNPP (Karenni National Progressive Party), while I waited at home for school to reopen.

"You're not going with us? Ka Paw Say! Why not?"

"Go *where*? I still have classes to attend."

Htoo, my classmate and a fellow college partier, wasn't himself when he visited me at my parents' home. In a protest march, he had linked arms with students and

LENS OF THE SHEPHERD

Buddhist monks and then watched friends imprisoned by surly Burma Army soldiers.

Htoo's raging purpose filled my parents' living room and turned my excuses to rat droppings. He glanced furtively at the door.

"Ka Paw Say! Everyone we know is joining the resistance. Everything has changed!"

I shook my head and didn't meet his eyes. "I don't want to fight our government."

"Don't be a coward. The Burma Army is killing our friends! If you are a man, you'll come with us."

I had never been interested in politics or human rights before. But, if I let Htoo leave to join the resistance without me, shame would dog my steps — a familiar cur that I despised.

"Are you a *man* or not?"

His insult brought me to my feet, and Htoo paused at the door.

I didn't tell my parents that I was leaving school to become a resistance fighter. That night I followed Htoo and other students down a narrow trail leading to a secret rendezvous known to cautious freedom fighters.

In the coming weeks, Mother, Father and my grandparents would quietly grieve over losing track of me. During prayer meetings at my parents' home, they would pray that I was still alive, while I lay upon a bed of leaves by candlelight, unlearning the government propaganda that teachers had thoroughly kneaded into my mind.

No one officially taught lessons to correct my view of

Karenni history. But at the primitive KNPP headquarters, I devoured the books that were made available.

It was the dry season, and I worked at the resistance camp with hundreds of other young men who trekked in from other states and divisions in Burma.

Many carried eyewitness accounts of Burma Army atrocities, and their stories reinforced everything that I was relearning.

After basic weapons training, I officially became a soldier with the Karenni resistance and immediately practiced the art of melting away in silent retreat. As expected, the Burma Army discovered the location of our headquarters and mounted an attack.

We moved our KNPP camp to the Pai River.

ॐॐॐ

At our new headquarters, officers ordered a school and church built for troops and families. Women and children lived along the Pai River, and our community continued to grow. The frontlines of our resistance war lay several miles away, and fresh troops left regularly after they received weapons training.

A Tatmadaw column marched like a mile-long centipede, devouring every village in its path.

Our Karenni resistance objectives seldom altered: A messenger informed the villagers ahead of the deadly juggernaut, to give them time to escape. After a cautious, judicial confrontation with the heavily armed battalion, our guerrilla snipers picked off Burma Army soldiers and planted mines along their route.

I eagerly waited for officers to order me to the front, where battalions of Tatmadaw soldiers most often controlled the high ground. I hungered to fire my M-16 in combat. I yearned to put my novice tactical training to the test. I volunteered for back-to-back patrols that scouted the passes and trails encompassing our headquarters. But *my* patrols never saw action.

A full year dragged by, snail-like, leaving a trail of discouragement in its wake. Sometimes soldiers returned to our Pai River headquarters, wounded in skirmishes. They described harrowing engagements, and I left their campfires, disgusted. I hadn't dodged a single bullet or fired my rifle at a Burma soldier!

And when I crowded into the front row of my unit, waiting expectantly as steely-eyed officers chose reinforcements to replace casualties, they completely skipped me!

Melancholy enfolded me like a heavy cloud, and finally I gave up my M-16 for a schoolteacher's instruction manual.

Our military leaders rated an educated man as valuable as any soldier. War-ravaged Karenni and Karen children were growing up ignorant of their own history, and displaced fathers and mothers had few tools or time to replant hopes and dreams in young hearts. Parents cherished hardy men and women who sat in cold huts teaching students science and mathematics.

But teaching school was only my *day* job.

"More wounded are coming in, Ka Paw Say! Get beds ready!"

A well-respected cousin had opened a medical clinic at the Pai River headquarters, and I assisted him in treating patients. While teaching school, bandaging injured soldiers and helping deliver babies, I began to slowly shed years of self-centeredness. I even reconnected with my parents through letters home.

I believed that life had busted me to a rock-bottom rank, but in reality, God was forging purpose in my heart where none had ever survived. For four long years the hammer rang on the anvil, shaping me for work as a Free Burma Ranger.

❧❧❧

The Burma Army successfully shelled our headquarters again — barracks, school, church and IDP camps — to charred rubble. I retreated with KNPP units, then stayed with family members for a time.

KNPP officials, who knew my aptitude for administration, transferred me to the Karenni Foreign Ministry office, and I thanked God for answering my prayer to learn about computers — until my instructor never showed up. My dream of computer training drifted in the bureaucratic mists for months.

Suddenly, I asked the blasphemous question that had nibbled at my soul whenever I curled up in an emotional foxhole: *Does God exist at all?*

LENS OF THE SHEPHERD

If he did exist, he certainly was wasting my time.

I worked on the Thai/Burma border a few rutty, muddy miles from bamboo "cities" with tens of thousands of Karenni and Karen refugees. A white missionary often visited these refugee camps and conferred with our Foreign Ministry on how best to help the displaced people still hiding in the Burma jungle.

Harboring great anger and hopelessness, I shook Dave Eubank's hand perfunctorily, unaware that God — whom I doubted even existed — was about to unveil the next phase of *his* training program for me.

Mustered Out, Deployed In

I awakened to my life's calling through two major events in 1997. At a Karenni refugee camp, I met beautiful Naw Po Gay, who would later become my wife. The second event launched me like an RPG into God's service, answering my need for lasting friendships and true purpose.

Without my knowledge, two officials in the Karenni government pointed me out to Dave Eubank as a "shy but good man," able to handle important work.

"This is the opportunity you've been waiting for, Ka Paw Say. Fill out these forms, and give them back to me." The head administrator at the Foreign Ministry office held out paperwork titled: Asian Institute of Christian Communication. I felt the hairs on the back of my neck stand up, like someone trained an M-16 at my chest.

"But, sir, it … it's all in *English*."

"Use a dictionary," he said and turned on his heel.

Each year, men and women from all over Asia — many holding Masters and PhDs — received technical training in radio, television, video recording, copywriting and other forms of communication at the celebrated AIC. And the common language used on all applications and at the conference was English.

I had left school before graduating 10th grade. I had less than two years of college, and my major was *partying*. My English skills included more hand signals than words.

Suddenly, I needed God to be real.

"Lord, I appreciate this, but you know I can barely read English. I'll do what I can, but chase this opportunity away, please!"

I struggled to fill out some of the form, but when I deciphered questions about my education, I grew irritated and stuffed the time-sensitive application between some books on a shelf. I had no interest in communications, and I planned to let the deadline sneak past.

But the next day, all three pages magically appeared on my desk!

The director paused as he passed by me. "Young man, get this filled out and *sent*."

When he left, I scribbled my signature on the bottom of the form. Then I folded it up, stuffed it in an envelope and dropped it in outgoing mail.

Some secretary at the AIC will tear up my half-completed application.

A few days later, I received a response.

It read: "Congratulations, Ka Paw Say! We look forward to seeing you at the Asian Institute of Christian Communications. Please send us the enclosed confirmation letter to verify your attendance."

The pesky opportunity follows me like a stray dog!

I felt a little weak in the knees. I glanced around at the empty office, panicked, then felt reassured — thank God, no one had seen me open the RSVP letter. I stuffed it deep into the trash can once and for all, to abort my chance of attending the mortifying conference.

A week later, I received my final communiqué from the AIC, and I opened the envelope cautiously. A shiver crawled up my back when a check for plane tickets dropped out.

God?

Dave Eubank had been in charge of vetting AIC applications at his headquarters. When he received my signed application, he surmised that my botched attempt to complete the questionnaire was due to my poor English, so he filled in the blanks for me! He based his answers upon reports of my past performance as a soldier, medic and teacher. He delivered my *fully completed* application to the institute with his endorsement.

A week later, Dave was alarmed that he hadn't received my attendance confirmation letter. And he wasn't about to let faulty mail delivery keep a good man from God's calling. He confirmed my seat at the conference and authorized payment for my two-way plane ticket!

Karenni Deputy Foreign Minister Doh Say booked my flight, and everyone at the Foreign Ministry office celebrated my all-expense-paid trip for communications training, while I withered inside.

"Ka Paw Say from the Karenni State in Burma" had never been issued any official identification in his whole life! I tried one last maneuver to avoid the inevitable shame I believed waited for me when I made a fool of myself among English-speaking students at the conference: In the country where the conference was held, local police rabidly profiled plane passengers, by checking IDs and travel papers. Before I arrived at the airport, I begged God — whom I finally acknowledged must be engineering this plot — *for mercy.*

"Jesus, before I board the plane, send the police to arrest me and take me to jail. Please, Lord."

Throngs of passengers waited to board, but I could only find *one* policeman. I pushed my way to stand in front of him, staring into his face expectantly, but he looked me over and yelled impatiently, "Do you have your ticket!?"

I was ready to confess anything, but he yelled again, "Get on the plane! You'll miss your flight!"

I was too stunned to argue with the policeman — or with God.

Something is going on here.

At the conference, I prayed that no one would strike up a conversation with me for the first week, while I learned as much English as possible.

God answered *that* prayer.

In roundtable groups, I struggled to understand my colleagues and our assignments. Finally, I broke down and asked God to send me help.

"Brother, do you comprehend the instructions?" asked an observant, helpful woman speaking impeccable English. She rescued me.

During the last half of the conference, while my fellow students slept each night, I worked late to complete my assignments. Our teams were learning how to communicate Christian values to Buddhists, Muslims, Animists and Atheists in Burma, using modern mediums of communication.

By the end of the courses, I was amazed that I had the confidence and ability to help my team members with *their* assignments! It was the first time in my life that I prayed consistently, and desperately, and I recognized God's voice motivating me to help others.

ও০ও০ও০

In 1997, the SPDC (State Peace and Development Council) in Rangoon (Yangon), the ruling junta that commanded the Burma Army at the time, ordered a massive scorched-earth offensive against their own people. Like a monsoon flood, Karenni, Shan and Karen IDPs swamped refugee camps in other countries. While the Tatmadaw attempted to purge the frontier of resistance groups and their sympathizers, the Free Burma Rangers emerged as a fledgling relief organization.

After my improbable triumph at the communications institute, I yielded my heart to the One who made it possible for me to succeed. I never doubted the existence of God again, but instead, questioned what I must do to fulfill my destiny.

Like my grandfather, I began visiting churches at the refugee camps and comforted the men and women severed from their homes and families. Doh Say, a well-known resistance fighter who worked at our Karenni Foreign Ministry, encouraged me to train as a missionary to IDPs.

In those early days, the Free Burma Rangers had little time to simulate mortar attacks or teach tourniquet techniques. Every mission Dave Eubank led was a forced march. His training program was "on the job," packing food and medical supplies behind hardcore Karenni, Shan and Karen guerrillas who knew where displaced families tried to survive until they reached the safety of refugee camps.

Dave encouraged able-bodied men and women that he met in the city or refugee camps to join his crusade to save the IDPs. He wrung from novice Rangers every sweaty drop of command potential they possessed. Most of us had no idea that we could lead rescue missions right under the noses of Tatmadaw battalions.

Through Dave Eubank, God struck flint to our latent potential, while physical and mental challenges fanned our abilities to brilliant flame.

On a wet December day in 1988, I hiked with the Free

LENS OF THE SHEPHERD

Burma Rangers for the first time to find IDPs who hid in the Karen mountains. Doh Say helped arrange for me to accompany the Rangers to document human rights violations.

Our destitute ethnics at refugee camps suffered with no electricity, no indoor plumbing, little privacy and plain rice for most meals. In the refugee camps, tiny bamboo huts withstood the monsoon winds and rain that pounded on tin or thatched roofs.

Refugees were taught to follow strict rules for sanitation, and any Burma refugee who needed a vaccine waited in long lines to see a medic or nurse. Life as a refugee was hard, but not intolerable.

But life as an IDP was nearly *unbearable.*

My fingers ached with cold as I trained my camera lens on unimaginable suffering in the Karen mountains. Families huddled in bamboo lean-tos like drenched chickens, praying to survive the wet months ahead.

I entered a shelter where a campfire in the center of the room wheezed and spat, stinging my eyes with a sickening human potpourri of diseases. A teenage girl tossed wet branches on the fire and sat near her father, who was dying from an undiagnosed fever.

With her father and mother, the girl had joined neighbors who fled to the hostile mountains. Even in the smoky half-light, my camera caught the hopelessness in the face of her mother, who meted out rice once a day from grain harvested before the Tatmadaw burned their fields.

The man would soon be dead, but his wife carried a more horrific fear within — that cruel soldiers might find their daughter in these unforgiving mountains.

Word spread among the IDPs that relief workers had come to treat their injuries and illnesses, and families slowly emerged uneasily from the jungle in small groups. For hours their heart-wrenching stories assaulted my recorder and lens.

After documenting their personal tragedies, cleaning infections seemed a cheerful task. As night fell, our infirmary emptied, and we weary medics and assistants crawled into wet sleeping bags and tents. We posted guards at our camp perimeter.

I felt a little ashamed that I wasn't inhaling the same diseased air that IDPs breathed in their shelters — then my prayers turned to snores.

The next morning, I helped chop through a mat of roots to dig graves for two men who had died of landmine injuries. We dug latrines, too, and offered detailed instructions about life-saving personal hygiene. The families took our warnings seriously, but we knew that they fought a losing battle. Almost everyone in the camps suffered from dysentery to some extent. Where did keeping clean fit on the survival scale? Every moment was taken up with scrounging everything edible, assembling shelters, cutting firewood and caring for drenched, miserable children.

We left the IDPs almost all our rice and medical supplies, and with near-empty packs, we followed Karen guerrillas past a Tatmadaw battalion that prepared to wreak havoc on more Karen farmers.

Along our muddy trail home, a personal call to bring help, hope and love to my countrymen and women gripped my heart. My first foray into Burma to help IDPs changed me forever.

The following year, Dave Eubank asked me to help him train Rangers with my skills in communications and to lead a mission to rescue and encourage IDPs.

In 2001, Naw Po Gay and I exchanged our marriage vows at Refugee Camp 5 with my friend and commander Dave Eubank officiating.

For 15 years, I have served as a relief worker and videographer with the Free Burma Rangers. For the Christians among thousands of IDPs I have cared for, I am their pastor. For my respected Free Burma Rangers — I am a shepherd and friend.

The Unflinching Camera

In 2003, I helped five Free Burma Rangers teams train to deploy to the Karen/Karenni border with relief supplies to aid thousands of IDPs.

At our training camp we reproduced scenarios to simulate working conditions during and after Burma Army attacks: evasive maneuvering, landmine removal, first aid, communications, evacs ...

After graduating our fresh-faced Rangers, we marched with heavy packs to the frontline areas to assist fleeing

IDPs and gather firsthand reports of human rights violations.

"Sleeping soldiers" (landmines) hid on well-traveled routes waiting to maim or kill us before we reached the IDPs. Karen guerrillas helped us dismantle the landmines and clear the trails so our caravan of porters and Rangers could safely pass.

It took us three days to reach the Karen/Karenni border where, just inside the Northern Muthraw District (Karen State), 1,000 people gathered in a chaotic community of need. We set up our pole-and-canvas medical clinic, while more families trickled in from the jungle around us, swelling our destitute flock.

Hundreds of IDPs lined up for treatments, and from a bird's eye view, our sprawling camp must have looked like an untidy colorful quilt — each patch filled with a sick or wounded child, man or woman.

Our new FBR staff joined experienced hardcore medics to treat 800 IDPs, one by one.

At night, scores of cooking and warming fires flecked the encampment. People slept wherever they could find space, thankful to feel safe and accepted, with a few armed guerrillas and us Rangers with them. For one of the dozens of pregnant women there, our nurses delivered a baby boy by flashlight.

Throughout the week, we handed out food, clothing, blankets, educational supplies and Good Life Club packets. The camp settled into a routine of sorts, and our Good Life Club swelled to hundreds as we old soldiers strummed guitars, sang and danced with abandon with the children. They wanted us to sing the same songs, like "Jesus Loves Me," over and over, and we did!

I wandered through the IDP camp with my camera, recording the testimonies of people who had suffered at the hands of Tatmadaw soldiers. Then someone told us about Ka Lae Lo, a village about five miles away that had been burned and looted. We decided to hike to the village to document the sad scene.

"They burned two of our barns full of rice! How will we survive now?" a Ka Lae Lo woman asked us.

We had no answer, except: "Trust God, and get your family across the border!"

Some called the Burma refugees "birds in a cage," because governments ordered all refugees to remain in the overcrowded camps. Relief organizations fed and cared for most of them.

But after months of hiding and foraging in the jungle, Burma refugees thought of their small bamboo houses as sanctuaries! And always in the back of their minds, the refugees hoped that they might someday return to Burma, their *home.*

The SPDC now controlled much of the Karen and Karenni border region so that their soldiers could safely work on building new roads. Most villages had been destroyed to ensure that no guerrillas could resupply.

Soon the SPDC would bring in loaders and loggers to clear-cut the ancient teak forests. Trucks would use the new roads to haul tin and tungsten ore from strip mines to the rail yards. Villagers were told that they would be shot on sight if they remained in this proposed industrial black zone.

It was about noon at Ka Lae Lo, and I had just interviewed a traumatized man who had been tortured by the Tatmadaw. Suddenly an explosion from the main trail sent chills up my spine. I knew the ugly timbre of a MM-2 landmine. The Burma Army often salted beaten paths with explosives to discourage families from going home.

Several young people had been sneaking back to Ka Lae Lo to scavenge through the charred remains. A teenage boy had touched off an antipersonnel device. The force of the blast sent 17-year-old Saw Sa Lu several feet off the trail, where his friends gathered him up to try to save him.

When we caught up with the frantic teenagers, Eliya Samson, our chief medic, quickly assessed the boy's blast trauma. A KNU (Karen National Union) medic bent in to help, and my gut ached as I switched on the camera.

The explosion had pulverized Saw Sa Lu's foot. Shattered bone remained connected to his upper right leg by a strip of flesh. I held my camera with sweaty hands as Eliya twisted a tourniquet tight and set up an IV bag, which he handed a boy to hold above Saw Sa Lu. The 17 year old was delirious, and his friends held a shirt close to his chin, blocking the gore from his eyes and memory.

"Hold him still," Eliya said quietly. He delivered local anesthesia and began the grueling task of isolating each slippery blood vessel and artery to suture them sealed. Saw

LENS OF THE SHEPHERD

Sa Lu's arm had suffered serious injury, too, and Eliya sutured these raw-looking flesh wounds as well.

At the end of the surgery, about eight inches of shin bone protruded below Saw Sa Lu's knee, barren of any flesh. Eliya and the KNU medic gently bandaged his boney stump, while we cut a bamboo pole and attached a hammock beneath it. Saw Sa.Lu groaned as Dave and Shannon, a missionary dentist, loaded him into the makeshift litter. They shouldered either end of the pole, swinging Saw Sa Lu between them in the sling. Another young man tied the IV to a bamboo stalk and held it above their friend as we all headed down the trail.

This is how we carried the wounded young man five miles, over streams and rocky hills, back to the IDP camp. After stabilizing Saw Sa Lu's vital signs, men carried him for four more days to a clinic with proper facilities to finish amputating the residue of his lower leg. Since its opening in 2003, the Hpa-an Orthopedic Rehabilitation Centre in Burma's Karen State has equipped some 7,000 amputees with prosthetic limbs.

Two-thirds of these amputees are landmine victims.*

God steadies my hands and steels my mind when my lens exposes soul-less and often vile scenes for the eyes of the world. To film and edit a story takes thoughtful immersion, and after a shoot, my personal history is reflected in every frame.

---

*The Economist, June 2013

In my life, Jesus has edited every crisis to show himself *real,* so that I can confidently tell my own story. Now I am a father of four children, and I pray that someday we can reunite with my family who lives in a Tatmadaw-controlled region of Burma. In the past 24 years, I have seen my father once and my mother two times. They are proud of the man I have become.

My wife, Naw Po Gay, worries when I follow Karen or Karenni guerrilla fighters to document Tatmadaw savagery. But she understands why I go. She was an IDP, too.

৵৵৵

Today, I train hundreds of Rangers of many faiths the art of visually telling stories about our courageous Rangers and the internally displaced people in Burma.

I shepherd these men and women, while my own odyssey of faith echoes in every report and video that circles the globe.

I hold my camera steady on little blond missionary girls singing and capering down a steep trail. A child's voice narrates: "My name is Sahale, and ... my dad helped start the Free Burma Rangers ... My mom, my sister, (Suuzanne), my brother, Peter, and I go into Burma to bring help and love to people under attack ... We want to tell the children that they are not forgotten."

CHAPTER 7
UPROOTED TO SERVE
SAW SUN'S STORY

"I could have easily stepped on a landmine or been shot many, many times ... In urgent moments you can cry out to God, and he will save you quickly."
Saw Sun — Team Coordinator, Nyaunglebin District, Karen State, Free Burma Rangers

Escape and Survive

Stay close! Run, children!
Our village, Nya Mu Kwee, was burning.

Sixty-millimeter mortars whistled above our heads. Grandmother leaned on her bamboo staff as she herded my sister and brother away from our house.

Auntie trotted after her with a bushel basket of rice and cooking pots jouncing against her back. The narrow basket's taut strap creased her forehead as she braced into each stride.

Naw Plaw Htoo, my mother, followed behind, carrying another basket filled with school supplies, a heavy family Bible and a few keepsakes. And she carried me — her second son — inside her belly.

Mom hated to think about the bombs gouging out Grandmother's lovely vegetable garden. On the trail leading to the village of Kokalo, she plodded along, while explosions drowned out the screams from our village. Naw Plaw Htoo prayed that her neighbors might escape before the Tatmadaw soldiers marched in to plunder and kill.

Word had reached Burma Army commanders that families of KNU (Karen National Union) resistance fighters were living in the Hsaw Htit Township — *and it was the season to burn their nests.*

A lookout had observed Tatmadaw soldiers positioning high-angle mortars on a hillside aimed at Nya Mu Kwee. A barefoot boy lugging an M-1 had warned my mom, grandmother, my auntie and my siblings, "You need to leave now! Hide!"

Nine months earlier, my father had been home briefly, then returned to the frontlines to defend our Kler Lwe Htu District. Mom was proud of her husband, Karen leader Saw Win Maung, yet at times like these, she wished he was just a farmer.

But where could a husband plow his fields and plant rice anymore?

Father's land had been confiscated after the military government nationalized all resources and land. The Union of Burma now claimed all private property in the Karen State, and villagers could either grovel before the Burma Army or resist.

Saw Win Maung and many others chose to resist.

UPROOTED TO SERVE

My father was a seasoned KNU fighter when he fell in love with my mother and married her. And though they hated to be apart, my parents shared a higher calling than just raising a family. Each crusaded against tyranny in his or her own way.

In his youth, Father had chambered rounds alongside hardened guerrillas. By his mid-30s, he led battalions.

My mom never graduated from high school, but she challenged neighborhood women to bring their children to her for an education. Naw Plaw Htoo handed out sticks of charcoal to cipher with and taught students about their Karen heritage and culture.

Father risked his life at the frontlines to win independence for his Karen people. Mom used her teaching gift to instruct her own children and others about a God of justice and love.

When Father struggled over leaving his family with relatives or friends to return to the frontlines, he explained his convictions this way: "I am fighting for *all* Karen people. Not just my family. And someday, we will all enjoy freedom together."

But where was her soldier now?

Rain soaked my mother — and her sarong suddenly felt *warm*. She stopped and kneeled on the ground, holding her breath.

"Is it time?" Grandmother asked, and Auntie grabbed a soaked blanket and spread it above Mom like a little banyan tree.

"Help your auntie!" Grandmother ordered, and my

brother and sister held a loving, dripping canopy above me.

Black smoke boiled from the direction of our village, and I slipped into my old midwife's gentle hands on the trail to Kokalo — a born freedom fighter.

My grandmother cleaned my face and handed me to Mother. She severed my umbilical cord and smiled at us.

Naw Plaw Htoo stood up with me in her arms, testing her resolve with a few steps. She nodded to Grandmother and Auntie who wrapped arms on either side of her shoulders.

"Oh, God. May he survive all this," Mom prayed. "And keep his father safe."

Trickles of rainwater carried her tears away.

We reached Kokalo and discovered that almost all the inhabitants had run away. They were expecting a visit from the Tatmadaw, too. My splintered family followed other IDPs to a hide site deep in the jungle and cut bamboo poles to build a thatched shelter. There were edible roots and fruit in the jungle, if you knew where to look.

సౌసౌసౌ

God always helped my mother find villages that would accept our family whenever we were displaced by the Burma Army. Buddhist villagers were often kind and helpful. Animists, who worshiped spirits, were sometimes aloof. Christians were usually generous.

But no matter who helped us survive, we knew that they sacrificed their own meals so that we could eat. Mother used her ability as a teacher to earn a portion of rice and sometimes a roof over our heads. Sometimes we stayed for months in a village, doing chores and helping any way we could.

A few days after I was born, we found another village in our Kler Lwe Htu District and lived there for a whole year, until the Tatmadaw came again. It was right before rice harvest.

A Burma Army officer had surprised the headman at his home, and while soldiers harshly interrogated him, we disappeared into the jungle. Mom always kept survival go-baskets of food and necessities ready. Other villagers joined our little caravan as we tramped away from certain death or abuse.

Several minutes from the village, voices sent us scurrying off the trail to crouch in thick underbrush crawling with insects. Smoldering bamboo and the sharp smell of burning flesh filled the evening air, and shots rang out in the distance.

A platoon of armed Tatmadaw trackers guffawed as they stomped casually into view.

Women would be ill-used when captured. Men would be hauled off to become human pack animals. We must be deathly still.

Children in our group rustled leaves. Parents squeezed their shoulders in warning. I wriggled in my mother's arms, whimpering, and Grandmother placed her calloused, comforting hand against my cheek. A man beside Mom glowered down at me, fingering his machete.

I gathered up a deep breath before a hungry wail but sighed instead. Mother satisfied my complaint by nursing me.

I happily ignored everyone's fearful eyes clamped on me.

Keep Saw Sun quiet. Please, Jesus. Please, Mother prayed silently.

Our band of IDPs stared after the Burma Army soldiers like they were prowling tigers, and we stayed in hiding long after they were out of sight. I was sound asleep when Naw Plaw Htoo and family discovered a hide site where villagers of many faiths gathered to pool resources and *survive.*

❧❧❧

In these chaotic times, men were forced to take sides in our war for freedom. Almost all Karen villagers were supporters of the resistance movement in some way and lived under terror that the Tatmadaw knew this.

As homes in the Kler Lwe Htu District were systematically ransacked and burned, our jungle camp swelled. Untrained Karen soldiers armed with machetes rotated at intervals to guard the perimeters of our hidden communities. We shared talents. A builder helped erect bamboo shelters, and a wood carver made utensils and bowls. A hunter killed monkeys or trapped birds for food.

Singers sang, and storytellers wove their yarns, while women braided baskets. Some men built Buddhist shrines for their worship. Christians gathered in bamboo churches thatched with palm fronds.

In most communities, my mother was respected because she was an educated woman. She requested that schools be built, and she enlisted women to lace tight-woven mats for students to use like chalkboards. If no building was available, and it was raining, she taught us under some thick-leaved tree, as best she could.

Our nightmare recurred whenever the Tatmadaw found our hidden communities. Escaping to the jungle meant starting over again in a new place, facing new dangers. Wild boars, tigers, feral dogs, pythons and water buffalo slithered and roamed about, and amoral men justified their thievery as *surviving.*

After a Tatmadaw offensive, Mom might spend weeks trying to find a village that would accept new people. Often she stood at someone's door, like a thin little child, begging for rice, while being scolded and threatened. Sometimes it was a language barrier that kept us from receiving a few handfuls of rice for our meal. Sometimes it was *fear.*

But God always sustained us. When villages rejected us, banana trees fed us. When people sent us packing, my mother would stumble upon nourishing roots for us to harvest and eat.

One day Mom left us kids at a river's edge while she foraged for jungle fruit, and we spied a beautiful stand of sugar cane! We skittered to it like hungry rodents and hacked it to pieces, happily sucking out the nectar, its sugary sap sticking to our fingers.

But it wasn't sugar cane. It was a river weed, transformed by our great imaginations.

These were desperate times for my mother, and whenever she met a Karen soldier who served at the front, she asked after company commander Saw Win Maung.

And she tasked them to carry word back to my father: Naw Plaw Htoo was waiting for her beloved commander to come *home*.

Big River

I was 8 years old when we moved farther east, where we knew no one. We stayed for a time among generous people who shared their rice. It seemed that everyone had enough food, because the Tatmadaw hadn't launched a major offensive in their area yet.

Mom knew it was just a matter of time before the Burma Army stripped these prosperous farmers of their livelihoods. It was too close to the main roads to be *safe*. Mom packed us up, and we trekked farther into the jungle to a valley beside a big river full of fish.

Just a few families lived at the village on the Big River, and exactly as my mother predicted, the Burma Army plundered the farms on main trails. Soldiers burned homes and butchered livestock to feed battalions and stole men to work on road-building projects. Families that escaped struck out through the jungle, and some ended up settling along our Big River, too.

Our haven wasn't really safe all the time. Mom still kept our go-baskets handy, and every few months we fled to the jungle to hide, as battalions passed close by. We often buried food on various trails outside our camp, to dig up when we were hiding.

More and more Karen men wore KNU uniforms, and the guerrilla units that stopped to resupply at our village seemed more disciplined. Most were carrying M-16s now, and the new military structure impressed me. As our community grew, KNU soldiers stayed close to protect us, or at least warn us when the Tatmadaw was near.

During our three years on the Big River, our greatest thrill was when Commander Saw Win Maung and his contingent of KNU soldiers visited us. Our house was built close to the river, and we mobbed Father on the grassy bank, demanding stories and hanging on his every word. Mom prepared rice that we grew and harvested with other villagers, and Grandmother's garden flourished with herbs and spices. Curry and love flavored our home until Father had to leave. As he waved goodbye, his daughters wept, and Mom swiped at tears, too.

"Sit down, Saw Sun. It's time to study."

I hated it when Mom said that. I ran the riverbanks like a panther, clutching a bamboo "M-16" and playing war with other boys, who also dreamed of becoming resistance fighters. My father's rank assured that I was usually the leader of troops in our mock battles.

Commander Saw Win Maung's presence never really left me. Respect, heroism and authority marked my family, and my mother wore these qualities like an officer's medals. My heritage followed me the rest of my life.

֎֍֎֍֎

"Saw Sun! We can't stay. Our soldiers are pulling back. Here, take this." Mother handed me rolled up sleeping mats as I counted everyone. We were all together, ready to run, *again*. Gunfire echoed across the valley, and 30 KNU soldiers held off Tatmadaw troops pouring along the banks of our Big River like angry red ants.

A panicked, bleeding water buffalo bellowed in agony as it ran by. Bullets pattered the jungle like rain on tin, and we ran like a deadly tsunami gathered behind us. We thrashed down a narrow, brush-choked trail, while mortars began shaking the ground.

The Burma Army officers had scheduled the burning of our village just before the rice harvest in May. Now there was no chance that we could resupply KNU troops, let alone feed ourselves through the year. For two days, we walked, until we found a place suitable for building shelters.

And we were *home*.

I helped men cut trees for posts to elevate our bamboo shelters above snakes and high water. Some of the men hunted boar to share with families who hadn't brought food. We gathered palm fronds for roofing, and weavers went to work braiding up walls and room dividers.

Our farmers cleared and cultivated land for planting rice right away to harvest in November or December, barring floods, blight or enemy soldiers.

I was 11 years old then, but we had to move again when I was 12.

It was different when the Tatmadaw soldiers found us this time. We had no livestock to kill, and they didn't seem as interested in burning down our homes. Instead, they shot as many people as they could find, in cold blood. Something had changed in their orders handed down by military leaders in Rangoon.

Wipe all resistance out.

Mom gathered her brood, and we fled into the jungle again. We children were older now and helped her forage for roots and bananas wherever we bedded down for the night. We knew that Father was fighting for his life somewhere, too, and we prayed for him every day. Mom still carried our big family Bible, tattered but legible, and she read verses to us each evening if we had shelter or when it wasn't raining on the pages.

We moved back to a renovated village that we had evacuated years before and threw up a small house to live in. Mom laid out our bamboo mats, and we settled in like wary nesting birds, always ready to take flight. About twice a year, KNU lookouts warned us that the Burma Army marched near, and we vacated the house until the coast was clear again.

RANGERS IN THE GAP

For two years, I was privileged to attend a village school where Mother taught, until my father returned from the front one day. He had been promoted to higher rank and was able to break away to see us more often.

My parents sat down with me.

"Saw Sun. You're 14 now, and it's time for you to go to high school," Father said. "I know of a fine boarding school on the Salween River. About 1,000 people live in the village, and the KNU protects the academy grounds where you will stay."

It seemed strange to leave my vagabond lifestyle behind to live in a guarded, secure place for the next three years. But God had been preparing me. I spoke to Jesus every day now, and I knew that he was mapping out my destiny.

"And take this with you, Saw Sun."

Mom's hair had turned gray from years of worry over loved ones and narrow escapes. She handed me a small New Testament, and I wondered where she had been able to find one in the jungle.

"Read it every day," she said, and the three of us bowed our heads together.

I *knew* what I would do when I graduated. God willing, I would go to the frontlines to be with my father, Commander Saw Win Maung.

I had no idea that the frontlines of war would find *me*.

UPROOTED TO SERVE

Breaking In

Dorm life was exciting! So many students and so much to learn in my classes! And it wasn't all history, science and mathematics after all. I also learned to shoot and clean an M-16. We were schooled on basic frontlines conduct, like how to take cover in mortar attacks, obey orders promptly and stay out of the line of fire.

I attended school at the academy for two years, proud to be a part of our resistance stronghold. Like a Burma tiger, the KNU clawed deep to hold this Salween territory, and our monument to freedom stung the pride of the military junta in Rangoon.

In 1989, they sent Tatmadaw hordes to flay the tiger.

Carrying rice wrapped in palm fronds wasn't as exciting as shooting an M-16, but it was just as crucial to the men on the battle lines. I was in ninth grade and assigned with others in my class to weave my way through kill zones to deliver food to our troops. Between these chow runs, I carried ammo and equipment, while mortars shrieked above my head.

Determined Tatmadaw officers kept up a steady barrage of 60, 80 and 120mm mortars that twisted up vehicles and leveled houses. And Burma Army marksmen had identified our supply routes where I ran ammo night and day.

For 30 days, I watched our frontline arc back like a green bamboo stalk, then snap straight again, over and over. Unlike school children in democratic nations, we weren't running to score points for a pennant — we fought for our lives. We raced like rabbits across killing fields where the enemy lobbed mortars as fast as they could load them.

I ran the gauntlet several times a day, but this time my load of ammo seemed heavier than usual as I hurried behind a friend who followed a group of soldiers.

Out of the gloom, a 120mm mortar round landed somewhere and splattered mud and dirt in my face. My ears rang, and I got to my feet, wiping grime from my eyes — and that's when I perceived his screams.

My friend's knee no longer joined his shin and thigh. Only a pulpy mass held them together. A soldier ahead of him lay silent, his hip partially hollowed out.

It took a few seconds for my mind to wake up. Uninjured soldiers on the trail ran back to tourniquet my friend, and medics seemed to magically appear in the confusion. Soldiers loaded the two casualties on litters to be transported away from the front.

I took nothing for granted after that, while I beat a path across the kill zone every few hours.

I prayed every time.

We celebrated a short-lived victory after the Burma Army retreated. Their 30-day blitz had failed. In the coming months, I graduated and left my boarding school to focus on military training at the KNU headquarters.

In the same year that I waved goodbye to my friends from a departing troop truck, the Tatmadaw invaded again. They overwhelmed our KNU forces with superior troop strength and firepower. The academy grounds and dorm of my alma mater have been in the hands of the Burma Army since that time.

ॐॐॐ

My father was a teenager when Karen guerrillas helped the British rout the Japanese invaders from our homeland. But after the British left — in a period of political intrigue and assassinations — a military junta led by a general named Ne Win built an Army to control all the resources and land in Burma.

Our Karen State leaders defied Ne Win and lost a pivotal battle to unseat the military regime at Rangoon (Yangon) in 1949. My father joined a fledgling insurgency committed to gaining full independence from the oppressive dictatorship. Our struggle for human rights and autonomy continues to this day.

Rummaging through my father's footlocker of wisdom, I treasure a gem that he left me before his march into eternity.

He knew I would face Tatmadaw bullets defending our Karen people. He told me, "Soldiers carry good luck charms, but luck has no meaning in war. All that counts during the battle is to be right with God. Even in hand-to-hand combat, or if a sniper fires a bullet at your head, God will save you. Son, to stay *safe*, stay pure in heart."

As a freedom fighter for more than 50 years, my father had never been wounded in battle. Some of his last words to my older brother and me were, "I have no inheritance to give you boys, except the resolve to free your people."

I cherish Commander Saw Win Maung's legacy and have done my best to bind virtue to my soul as he did.

At 17 years old, I joined the KNU to train for combat. I had excelled in my academic studies, including English, and after months of basic training, I spent time teaching, then marched to the frontlines to learn the art of jungle reconnaissance. In time, my fellow graduates and I stalked the enemy on silent, deadly patrols.

Teacher Soldier

"Stay in your position until the Burma Army moves again. Then rendezvous with us," our unit commander ordered as he left us.

Our sniper had killed a soldier on point, and confusion seized the Burma Army battalion wending along a jungle trail. The 300-man column seemed paralyzed, every man glaring at the green wall of jungle on either side of him.

"They look like pigs waiting for their throats to be cut," someone whispered.

A half-dozen of us were painted into the landscape like chameleons. We listened to a Burma Army patrol thrashing through the jungle trying to pick up our sniper's trail. But in less than an hour, they returned to their fuming officers without a kill.

They had planned to brutalize the villagers a couple miles ahead, but now, only bamboo huts remained to visit their rage upon. Our mission had been successful: Our network of Karen freedom fighters delayed the Burma Army battalion long enough for the villagers to gather their families and *run*.

Before I soldiered on the frontlines, I joined my mother in a campaign against another foe that killed more people in Burma than the Tatmadaw. *Ignorance*. My mother and I taught subjects ranging from hygiene to history at the KNU headquarters and surrounding villages. The Burma Army had been systematically purging village schools, recognizing that passionate teachers armed with truth could, in time, conquer them by spreading the hope of democracy. The future lay in the hearts of these bedraggled, intelligent students — the reformers of the next generation.

My mother had mentored hundreds of these IDPs over decades, and her charcoal sticks and bamboo tablets now filled *my* basket as a teacher-soldier.

ॐॐॐ

At the supreme headquarters of the KNU in 2001, God's gift to me — my education — sent me to the head of the line for computer training. Most of my patrols in those days amounted to helping my own family and completing paperwork for my superiors. It was a time of inner turmoil for me, as I groped for God's purpose in my life.

I was growing to understand that the Tatmadaw and ignorance were only tools in the hands of an evil force that held my country with an iron grip. Sadly, all my personal strategies to break this evil's hold seemed feeble, like guerrilla warfare — always defensive; shoot and run away. I was adept at harassing evil, but I yearned to *overcome* it! Killing Burma Army soldiers would never move my personal frontline of battle a single inch toward victory.

I was intrigued when a missionary who talked more like a soldier arrived at headquarters and grabbed the attentions of our busy district chairman and KNU officers. He and his hybrid relief teams called Free Burma Rangers requested assistance in locating jungle hideouts where IDPs subsisted. With little official help, they had already been packing in relief to thousands of Burma IDPs since 1997.

Dave Eubank's genuineness and logistical expertise elicited confidence from our leaders, and they sanctioned his radical plan to combine armed Karen security teams and Free Burma Rangers to "bring help, hope and love" to the desperate IDPs.

My commander ordered me to accompany Dave Eubank on the first relief mission, and I was only an observer tasked to help set up camps, haul supplies, cook and assist the medics.

Dave, 20 Rangers and I marched from their headquarters into the Nyaunglebin District, Western Karen State. Each of us carried 40- to 70-pound rucksacks full of medical equipment, rice, educational supplies and other necessities to help internally displaced people at what these Rangers called hide sites.

UPROOTED TO SERVE

Most of our Rangers carried no weapons, so we obviously counted on divine intervention to win in a confrontation with the Tatmadaw. Among these men, I immediately recognized the same brand of courage I saw in men at the front. Rangers slogged through mud and bandaged wounds like they were rushing machine-gun nests.

Shooting at the enemy had always fed my passion for immediate justice; *teaching* satisfied my motivation to inspire students to fight for freedom. But the Rangers' *souls* fought the battles at hide sites. On jungle trails, love overwhelmed the evil that I had been trying to fight with an M-16.

Even before our mission began, our commander, Dave Eubank, briefed us on FBR protocols: "If we run across a battalion, our imperative is to stay between the IDPs and the enemy. We never initiate a firefight. But we *never* surrender if they try to overrun us. We defend the IDPs to the last man."

Dave had accepted a yoke placed on his shoulders by Jesus, and his face glowed with pleasure as our work grew more arduous.

The last strand in the cord that bound me to the Free Burma Rangers and their way of fighting evil was their use of technology. Cameras peered into the hearts of IDPs. Rangers broadcast to nations everywhere what fear, hopelessness, torture, death and psychological abuse in Burma looked and sounded like.

IDPs depended upon God to motivate individuals and

organizations to intervene when outraged over the Burma government's genocide of ethnic people.

I wasn't the only Karen who felt frustrated at our lack of progress in defeating brazen tyranny. In 2001, our commanders weighed future strategies against past operations. Dave Eubank began intense briefings with ethnic leaders proposing a new game plan to enflame the international community and pressure the military junta toward democratic reforms. These were perilous times for the Eubank family, as Dave's powerful ideas rocked the jade mansions of military despots in Rangoon.

Scores of ethnic volunteers from as far away as the Kachin State were already flocking to Dave's call for medics, porters and security soldiers. They stood ready to march into the jungle with food and supplies, because many had families living as IDPs or refugees!

Dave's teams documented their relief missions with military precision to shine light into the jungle warrens where terrified IDPs subsisted. His team visually linked human rights abuses with the Burma government and circulated the information worldwide via the Internet. The Free Burma Rangers would seek partners to help bankroll relief drives. Dave called his good-news offensive: *"Overcoming Evil with Good."*

All Dave needed from the KNU was their endorsement, land for a training camp and help in protecting pack trains with supplies escorted by Rangers as they searched out starving families.

UPROOTED TO SERVE

New Way to Fight

My lifestyle changed overnight when the Karen National Union chose me to be their liaison with the Free Burma Rangers. Dave's new training camp in the Karen State challenged guerilla fighters to exchange M-16s for 50-pound rucksacks full of rice and medicines. At the Karen training camp, prayer in the name of Jesus Christ was essential, expected and never opposed, no matter one's philosophy. The overriding objective — bringing help, hope and love to the IDPs — permeated map and compass training, medical technique and rappelling courses. And from opening prayer on our first day until graduation ceremony, Dave pounded us with a maxim that he lived by: *Never give up.*

Soon ethnic leaders in several states and divisions began sending men and women for the dynamic Rangers training offered in the heartland of Burma. Some soldiers served on a single FBR mission and returned to their units. Others, like me, remained freedom fighters, but answered a call to fight a new way.

For 10 years, I have served my people as a Free Burma Ranger, and I *feel* the frontline of evil being pushed back when I cradle an orphaned child in my arms. Or watch teachers weep over school supplies spread on a tarp in a jungle clearing. Or when I listen to IDPs pouring out their stories of leaving homes behind *forever.* Their futures might appear hopeless, but they can count upon God's mercy — even in a monsoon on the trail to Kokalo!

෨෧෨෧෨෧

In 2008, Dave performed my wedding as I vowed to love, honor and cherish my beautiful fellow Ranger, Naw Paw Blu. Her name means "flower," and we march on jungle trails together serving God.

Burma's cavernous emotional and physical need turns everything normal upside down. Here, children often carry children away from danger. Mothers carry grandmothers, and fathers carry grandfathers who have no more strength to walk.

I have seen my Flower pack an exhausted elderly woman upon her back a great distance to deliver her for medical treatment. Naw Paw Blu has helped deliver babies, cared for children and assisted her Ranger team in hiding terrified IDPs from the Tatmadaw.

Like me, her strength and resolve is sustained by her daily relationship with and faith in Jesus.

෨෧෨෧෨෧

A few of us from our main Rangers team hid in a bamboo thicket, too far away to photograph Burma Army soldiers kicking through the ashes of Hti Baw Ta, a village in Ler Doh Township, in the Nyaunglebin District. The soldiers were under orders to locate and steal rice and other provisions that villagers had cached in the jungle. Hti Baw Ta was the second village targeted for incineration.

Our Free Burma Rangers team estimated that 2,100

villagers had been displaced to jungle hide sites while the battalions marched through the township. More than a dozen schools had been abandoned, and panicked children and teachers scattered like field mice. Three villagers were reported killed.

At one of the hide sites, a woman stifled her cries of pain. Medics and friends had constructed a three-sided screen of bamboo stalks and palm fronds for her privacy. A nurse spread a small plastic mat beneath her, and the pregnant mother lay with an arm across her face, as if to hide her soul from the world. Outside her lean-to, her three other children curled on palm-frond bedding, exhausted and sleeping fitfully.

A series of groans signaled the crowning of her baby boy, and then, he was *out.* Another Karen soldier? A teacher someday? A refugee?

For the moment, just a *son* and a little brother in a family bound for a refugee camp several weeks' journey away.

After more than half a century fighting bloody battles, my father would have been wary about our cease-fire agreement with the Union of Myanmar (Burma), allowing them safe passage through Karen lands. In fact, 10 of the 11 ethnic resistance groups in Burma have reached exploratory peace pacts with the government.

We Karen ethnics plot our futures as if hiking through landmine territory — *no* trail feels safe.

Since the peace agreement in 2012, the Tatmadaw grows ambitious, building and expanding bases to potentially control our Karen natural resources, like rice, rubber, teak and precious stones. We see fewer armed patrols on our roads, but villagers continue to suffer from the government's exacting schemes.

Only two months after the cease-fire was signed, in eight villages at the Doo Tah Htoo Township, the Tatmadaw officers ordered one villager from every family to work for their company, planting 500 acres of rubber plants. No laborers received wages at the plantation, and if a worker failed to show up, he was tracked down and thrown in prison.

Human trafficking of people forced into labor is also reported in other districts of the Karen State, like Dooplaya, where villagers are ordered to pull oxcarts full of wood to the Tatmadaw's Anankwin camp.

Who will hold the powerful Burma Army accountable for human rights abuses?

Seven years ago, the Tatmadaw stood guard while heavy equipment hollowed out 600 acres for the Toe Bo Dam in our Toungoo District. In 2013, farmers still live in a 2,000-acre floodplain below the dam. During the rainy seasons, muddy waters submerge their orchards and fields of mangosteen (a tropical fruit), coffee, lemon trees and rice.

Who will compensate farmers for their lost livelihoods?

My aging mother ended her teaching career about three years ago, and she tells stories to her grandchildren about our escapes and adventures in the Burma jungle. For the first time, Naw Plaw Htoo lives under the tentative peace of a cease-fire agreement — but she will always *feel* like an IDP. *Her go-baskets are stocked, and she is ready to run.*

Perhaps my mother will never feel true security until she is at home in heaven — but I work for her peace here on earth.

With support and prayers from friends in many nations, Free Burma Rangers continue to bring help, hope and love to our people. We pray for freedom and democracy in Burma, so that we all might live in peace.

POSTSCRIPT

In 1996, Dave Eubank's audience with democracy leader Aung San Suu Kyi at Inya Lake, Rangoon (Yangon), seemed as unattainable as holding the hand of Tatmadaw Army Major General Aung Min (Ret.) and praying with him.

But both meetings are miracles in the unfolding story of the Free Burma Rangers.

During the cease-fire agreement between the Burma central government and most of the armed resistance groups in Burma (Myanmar), present Minister of the President's Office, Aung Min, traveled to a city in a neighboring country to discuss a political prisoner release with the KNU (Karen National Union). On the day of the prisoner-release parley, Dave Eubank "happened" to be passing through the same city with his family and five Rangers.

In past years, either leader might have been targeted by snipers when their units met on a jungle trail. But here in an elegant conference center, God arranged a safe and poignant encounter between Dave and Minister Aung Min.

Dave had been 36 years old when he spoke to Aung San Suu Kyi about the future of Burma on his secret trip to Rangoon. He was 52 years old when he met with the

Minister of the President's Office Aung Min, in a conference atrium.

Their timely convergence included cordial introductions to Karen and Dave's three children. Minister Aung Min and Dave exchanged brief, but meaningful, words about their perspectives, and the minister invited Dave to Rangoon, as his guest — to gain insight.

Dave Eubank extended his hand to Minister Aung Min, and he took it. Then Dave prayed aloud: "Lord Jesus, I have no idea what to do next, and I believe that this man doesn't, either. But you have brought us together. Help us find your path into the future ..."

A strong sense of God's presence enveloped the two men as Dave prayed. Dave expressed later that he felt an unexpected warmth and openness from the Burma official.

As Dave turned to leave, no subtleties camouflaged his heart from Aung Min. The back of his jungle-green t-shirt read: *Love each other. Unite and work for freedom, justice and peace. Forgive and don't hate each other. Pray with faith, act with courage, NEVER SURRENDER.*

ৡৡৡ

At present, the Burma government's cease-fire agreement with 11 of 12 resistance groups remains alive, while political parties posture for Burma's general elections in 2015.

POSTSCRIPT

In the face of his own government's opposition, Minister Aung Min has advocated a change in the Burma constitution to allow democracy bellwether Aung San Suu Kyi, who won a seat in parliament in 2010, to run for president of Burma.* Under the current law, because her husband was foreign-born, she is not qualified to become a candidate for president or vice president.

Even if she does run for president, Suu Kyi faces an uphill battle to gain enough support in parliament to win in 2015. A president will likely be elected by a junta-weighted parliament, and not by the will of the general population.

And if Aung San Suu Kyi did win the election, would Burma's military generals relinquish their power and shape a reformed, democratic government?

Only God knows.

ॐॐॐ

On a major FBR mission in 2013, Saw Sun prayed that he wasn't leading his six teams into a deadly melee on the plains near the Sittaung River, along the Karen State border.

A single errant shot from an M-16 might erase the official truce and plunge them into a bloodbath. His young team members might be rounded up and shipped off to prison, never to be seen again.

---

* *The Irrawaddy*, April 2013

Most of his Rangers were fresh out of the six-week Free Burma Rangers training program, and Saw Sun marched them into a farm region cleared of secure, protective jungle cover. Here they planned to care for IDPs and villagers in plain sight of the Tatmadaw, based on the official but arbitrary cease-fire agreement.

Relocation villages approved by Tatmadaw overlords dappled the plains. The Burma Army controlled each relocation village from well-provisioned bases.

When word spread among the relocation villages that Free Burma Rangers delivered food and medical help to anyone in need, IDPs flocked to the FBR staging area.

And when Rangers threw the Good Life Club into high gear, Saw Sun sent messages to the Burma Army regimental commander, the battalion commander and the company commander: "We are the Free Burma Rangers, here to help people. We love everyone in Burma, including the Burma Army. Come see what we are doing. I invite you to our Good Life Club."

Hosting Burma Army officers had never been FBR standard operating procedure in any missions before. But by the end of their day with the Free Burma Rangers, the three Tatmadaw commanders had joined the Good Life Club.

Dave Eubank received Saw Sun's e-mail photos by satellite transceiver, *astonished*. Saw Sun stood with the Burma Army officers, each wearing a Free Burma Rangers t-shirt.

But in the wake of "help, hope and love," evil stalked

POSTSCRIPT

Saw Sun and his team. Some in the Burma Army bedeviled villagers, demanding that they refuse the Rangers' gifts. The picture of good was suddenly blurred as Saw Sun confronted the embarrassed regimental commander face to face.

"Sir, if you have a problem with how we run our program, please see me. Do not follow behind us and harass the people. You know we are doing *good*."

Since 1997, Free Burma Rangers have trained 260 teams, treated more than 500,000 patients and helped 1,100,000 people through relief efforts.

Teams continue to deploy in conflict zones or wherever IDPs are oppressed: in Burma's Arakan, Chin, Kachin, Karen, Karenni, Kayan, Lahu, Mon, Naga, Pa'O, Palaung and Shan regions.

In serving shoulder to shoulder with leaders like Saw Sun, FBR graduates adopt the Free Burma Rangers code into their souls: *Always* stand between oppressed people and evil, no matter the odds — and watch God deliver success.

Richard Drebert

CONCLUSION

Do you love my Jesus?

As you conclude this book, I want to encourage you to turn to Jesus. He wants to help you in all things, he is the answer to all problems. Each person in this story, as broken and sinful as he or she is, has found this to be true. We encourage you to pray to Jesus and ask him for whatever you need.

The beautiful people you've read about in this book don't sacrifice their comfort, their safety and even their lives because they are "good people." They do it because they passionately love a God who has placed HIS heart in theirs. Who has given them a heart transplant to see the world through his eyes. Who has given them a purpose and given them a calling to love, serve and REACH HIS CHILDREN who are hurting and mistreated on the other side of the world.

The work they do, the people they love, the way they work, the REASON THEY CARE is all because of the love of Jesus Christ.

Do you want a heart transplant today? Do you want to personally know a God who loves you so much that he sent his Son to die for you? Who loves HIS PEOPLE so much that he compels those who love HIM to cross oceans and borders so that THEY can love THEM? Who promises to remove the calloused heart that has been bruised and jaded by the world and give you a heart that beats in tune with his?

Admit that you make bad choices. Jesus Christ was the only person on the earth to live a life free from what the Bible calls sin. Romans 3:23 reads, "All have sinned and fall short of the glory of God." None of us, no matter how good we are or how hard we work or how much we attempt in our own strength to contribute to this world, is perfect. Every one of us finds ourselves striving to "be good" ... and daily falling short. None of us are "good enough" to be in the perfect presence of a sinless God.

Recognize that what you're doing isn't working. Accept the fact that Jesus desires to forgive you for your bad decisions and selfish motives. Realize that without this forgiveness, you will continue a life separated from God and his amazing love. In the Bible, the book of Romans, chapter 6, verse 23 reads, "The result of sin (seeking our way rather than God's way) is death, but the gift that God freely gives is everlasting life found in Jesus Christ."

Believe in your heart that God passionately loves you and wants to give you a new heart. Ezekiel 11:19 reads, "I will give them singleness of heart and put a new spirit within them. I will take away their stony, stubborn heart and give them a tender, responsive heart" (NLT).

Believe in your heart that "if you confess with your mouth that Jesus is Lord and believe in your heart that God raised him from the dead, you will be saved" (Romans 10:9 NLT). You are saved from a life eternally separated from him.

CONCLUSION

Believe in your heart that because Jesus paid for your failure and wrong motives, and because you asked him to forgive you, he has filled your new heart with his life in such a way that he transforms you from the inside out. Second Corinthians 5:17 reads, "When someone becomes a Christian, he becomes a brand new person inside. He is not the same anymore. A new life has begun!"

Why not pray now?

Lord Jesus, if I've learned one thing in my journey, it's that you are God and I am not. My choices have not resulted in the happiness I hoped they would bring. Not only have I experienced pain, I've also caused it. I know I am separated from you, but I want that to change. I am sorry for the choices I've made that have hurt myself, others and denied you. I believe your death paid for my sins, and you are now alive to change me from the inside out. Would you please do that now? I ask you to come and live in me so that I can sense you are here with me. Thank you for hearing and changing me. Now please help me know when you are talking to me, so I can cooperate with your efforts to change me. Amen.

David Eubank
Founder
Free Burma Rangers

GLOSSARY

8888: Burma's popular pro-democracy movement on August 8, 1988

AK-47: semi-automatic or automatic assault rifle used in Burma resistance

BA: Burma Army, also referred to as the Tatmadaw

Bamars: ethnic majority and ruling class of Burma

Battalion: in Burma Army, usually 200 to 300 soldiers

BSPP: Burma Socialist Program Party

C-130: known as the Hercules; a four-engine turboprop military transport

Company: 62 to 190 soldiers

De Oppresso Liber: means Free the Oppressed; Latin words on Special Forces insignias

DKBA: Democratic Karen Buddhist Army; broke from KNU in 1994; proxy Army of the SPDC

Dooplaya District: region in Southern Karen State

Dredge Holes: deep, muddy sludge pits left from ore diggings

Ethnics: Burma's people (other than Burmans), belonging to distinctive cultural, racial, religious or linguistic traditions

FBR: Free Burma Rangers; a multi-ethnic humanitarian service movement bringing help, hope and love to people in the war zones of Burma

Fish Paste: pungent, fermented pastes made of either fish or shrimp in Burma

Freedom Fighter: a person who battles against established forces of tyranny and dictatorship

GLC: Good Life Club; a relief arm of FBR aiding mothers and children in the displaced communities in Burma

Guerrilla: a member of an irregular armed force that combats stronger regular forces

Gulf War: (1991) war between US-led UN forces and Iraq, after Iraq's invasion of Kuwait

Headman: mayor

Hide Sites: locations where IDPs hide from the Burma Army

IDP: internally displaced person; individual who has been displaced from home but has not fled his or her country; that is, has not fled across an international border

GLOSSARY

Insurgency: insurrection/resistance by a group against a government

Karen: the Karen people, also known in Thailand as the Kariang or Yang, are an ethnic group in Burma and Thailand. Karen are the second largest population group in Burma after ethnic Burmese; the Karen have fought for independence from Burma since January 31, 1949

Karen State: traditional homeland of the Karen people, also known as Kayin State; control of the area is disputed between the military government of Burma and Karen groups, who refer to the area as Kawthoolei (Wikipedia)

KIO: Kachin Independence Organization

KNLA: Karen National Liberation Army; the KNU's armed wing since 1975

KNO: Kachin National Organization, pro-democracy Kachin organization

KNPP: Karenni National Progressive Party; Karenni pro-democracy resistance group

KNU: Karen National Union; pro-democracy resistance group in Karen State

Kyat: Burmese currency unit (abbreviated as "K"); official exchange rate: 1 USD = K 7; street rate: 1 USD = K 1240

Lotus: aquatic plant

M-1: a semi-automatic infantry weapon of the U.S. Army in World War II and Korean War

M-16: automatic or semi-automatic infantry weapon used by U.S. Army and in Burma conflict

M-79: 40mm single-shot breach-loaded grenade launcher

Mae Tha Ra Hta: ethnic nationalities of Burma met here to discuss internal peace, democracy, rights or national equality and self-determination for the ethnics and establishment of a genuine federal union

Mandalay: the second largest city and the last royal capital of Burma (Myanmar); it is the economic and cultural hub of Upper Burma (Wikipedia)

Mortar: a cannon very short in proportion to its bore, for throwing shells a distance at high angles

Mount Shucksan: a glaciated massif in the North Cascades National Park

Myanmar: Burma

Naypyidaw: the capital of Myanmar, north of Rangoon (Yangon); the capital's official name was announced on Burma Armed Forces Day in March 2006 (Wikipedia)

GLOSSARY

Ne Win: former Prime Minister of Burma for 26 years

NLD: National League for Democracy; main pro-democracy political party in Burma; led by Aung San Suu Kyi

Nyaunglebin District: region in Northeast Karen State

Ore: a metal-bearing mineral or rock, or a native metal that can be mined

Padamya: ruby

Palouse: major agricultural region in Southeast Washington State

Patrol: armed group of personnel assigned to monitor a specific geographic area

Platoon: approximately 16 to 44 soldiers in a unit

Powder Monkey: miner or construction worker, etc., who uses explosives

Rangoon/Yangon: the largest city and a former capital of Burma; although the military government has officially relocated the capital to Naypyidaw since March 2006, Rangoon/Yangon, with a population of four million, continues to be the country's largest city and the most important commercial center (Wikipedia)

Refugee Camps: camps not inside the refugee's country, mostly supported by relief organizations

Resistance: underground groups working as an opposing force to overthrow the occupying power

Rucksack: backpack

Shan: the Shan people are a Tai ethnic group of Southeast Asia; Shan people live primarily in the Shan State of Burma, but also inhabit parts of Mandalay Division, Kachin State and Karen (Kayin) State and in adjacent regions of China and Thailand; Shan are estimated to number approximately six million

SLORC: State Law and Order Restoration Council; official name for Burma's ruling military regime from 1988-1997

SPDC: State Peace and Development Council; the official name of Burma's ruling military regime from 1997-2011

Special Forces: branch of U.S. Army composed of soldiers specially trained in guerrilla warfare

SSA: Shan State Army; armed pro-democracy movement in Shan State

Tatmadaw: Burma Army

The Golden Land: name of Burma (Myanmar) known for its gilded temples

GLOSSARY

Toungoo District: region in Northern Karen State

Union of Burma: former official name of Burma

U.S. Army Rangers: elite Airborne infantry units in the U.S. Army

UWSA: United Wa State Army; proxy Army of the SPDC in the Wa State

Wai Greeting: slight bow, with the palms pressed together in a prayer-like fashion

NOTE
Information collected from: www.wikipedia.com and www.freeburmarangers.org

Moved by the stories you've read?
Want to make a DIFFERENCE?

HOW YOU CAN HELP:

Love each other.
Unite and work for freedom, justice and peace.
Forgive and don't hate each other.
Pray with faith, act with courage and never surrender!

1. Pray for the people of Burma and join in the Global Day of Prayer for Burma.
2. Encourage your government to help the people of Burma.
3. Work with your church, workplace or school to raise awareness of the situation in Burma.
4. Sponsor an FBR relief team.
5. Donate relief supplies or volunteer your time.
6. Organize a Run for Relief for Burma.
7. Donate financially:
   - At www.freeburmarangers.org
   - Through the Thai Christian Foundation
     Make a check payable to Thai Christian Foundation, designating FBR in a separate note.
     6116 N. Central Expressway, Suite 518
     Dallas, TX 75206
     The TCF tax ID is 75-1730295

For more information, visit www.freeburmarangers.org
or e-mail info@freeburmarangers.org.

ACKNOWLEDGEMENTS

I would like to thank Jeff Wall, senior pastor of Friends Community Church in Fairbanks, Alaska, for his vision for this book and his hard work in making it a reality.

And to Dave and Karen Eubank and the people of Free Burma Rangers, thank you for your boldness and vulnerability in sharing your personal stories. And to Hosannah Valentine, thank you for your generous assistance in helping us make this happen.

This book would not have been published without the amazing efforts of our Project Manager and Editor, Jeannette Scott. Her untiring resolve pushed this project forward and turned it into a stunning victory. Thank you for your great fortitude and diligence.

Deep thanks to our incredible Editor in Chief, Michelle Cuthrell, and Executive Editor, Jen Genovesi, for all the amazing work they do.

I would also like to thank our invaluable Proofreader, Melody Davis, for the focus and energy she has put into perfecting our words.

I also want to extend our gratitude to the creative and very talented Jenny Randle, who designed the beautiful cover for *Rangers in the Gap: Act with Courage. Never Surrender.*

And finally, our gratitude goes to author Richard Drebert, whose diligence and talent make this book difficult to put down.

Daren Lindley
President and CEO
Good Catch Publishing

For more information on reaching your city with
stories from your church, go to
www.testimonybooks.com.

GOOD CATCH
PUBLISHING

Did one of these stories touch you?
Did one of these real people move you to tears?
Tell us (and them) about it on our Facebook page at
www.facebook.com/GoodCatchPublishing.